The Code

The Code

THE CODE

Basics for Texting and Instant Messaging

John & Barbara Dorgan

First Edition June 2009

© Copyright 2008 Handy Tabs

Printed In The USA
Handy Tabs
4935 Spring Road
Oak Lawn, IL 60453

First Printing June 2009

All Rights Reserved. No part of this book may be used or reproduced in any manner without written permisson of the publisher, except for brief quotations in critical reviews or articles.

Design & Artwork By Amelia Leubscher
Edited By Michele Kampf
Special Contributions By Pamala Dorgan

ISBN 10-0615-27198-7
ISBN 13-978-0-615-27198-9

Library of Congress Control Number: 2009930279

This book is dedicated to caring and watchful Moms around the world, and especially to
Our Loving Mothers,

Anna Kampf-Fox

&

Louise Hall-Dorgan

Discernment is Mandatory

Mother taught us that most people are kind and giving; that the world is basically good; that people the world over want the same things... Family, friends, security, respect, and help in times of need. Though language may be a hurdle to understanding, human nature is not.

She also taught that, for whatever reason, a small amount of people are truly evil; and, even the best of us make mistakes. One of her classic pieces of advice is still with us to this day... "whenever someone, anyone, asks you to believe something, ask yourself what this person has to gain or lose by convincing you that this is true." This gain or loss test has served us well in putting so-called "facts" into proper perspective. Think about it whenever you are in a position of doubt. When your sixth sense tells you that something is wrong, trust your feelings. Mother couldn't have dreamed she was giving great advice for web users of today.

THE CODE IS "AMASSED"!

Are you perplexed by the shortcuts everyone uses for texting and instant messaging?

Until now you were unable to find one central location to translate **A**cronyms, **M**etaphors, **A**bbreviations, **S**ymbols, **S**imiles, **E**ncryptions and **D**o-fers, hence the acronym **"AMASSED"**. Oh how frustrating when you absolutely NEEDED to know.

On that basis, we created "The Code" ~ the quintessential easy reference you've been waiting for… in alphabetical order!

Contents

Dedication...5
Discernment Is Mandatory..........................6
Acknowledgement......................................10
Introduction...11
History Of Thumbers.................................14
Flagged Entries..18
Smileys..21
Morse Code...28
10-Codes...32
Phonetic Alphabet.....................................40
"Amassed" A To Z.....................................43
Beware! Webs Have Spiders....................146
World-wide Web Pitfalls...........................148
Protecting Your Children Online..............159
"Sexting"..164
Cyberbullying...168
Safe Thumbing...170
Your Brain on Twitter...............................173
Be Forgiving...177
Medical Alert..180
Metaphors For Drunk On Alcohol...........182
Metaphors For High On Drugs................184
Net Neutrality..188
Text-Ers & Instant Message-Ers...............190
Help Has Arrived.....................................191

Acknowledgement

Our Sincere Appreciation Goes To

Jeffrey Mathew Fox
Amelia Elizabeth Leubscher
Pamala Hall Dorgan
Kelley Anne Dorgan
Michael Daly
Jon & Jamie Dorgan
Bradley Janecek
David & Laura Simmons
Sarah Ward

and to those helpful individuals we interviewed, who gave the gift of their time and knowledge to help make this book more complete.

You have our gratitude.

Introduction

There's been considerable talk lately about text messaging, instant messaging, and the phenomenon it's becoming. We've only just started text messaging; mainly because it's just easier for us to pick up the phone and talk. We hadn't yet grasped the concept of texting for fun or necessity. Being neophyte "thumbers", we complained about how difficult it was when you don't know the lingo.

One evening, Jeff, one of our brothers, called to share another of his many ideas with us. After listening to his adult children talk about text messaging, he had an idea about compiling an organized reference guide of popular acronyms that are used frequently on cell phones and online. He urged us to write that guide. Coincidently, we just previously had our own conversation on the same subject, so we all recognized the need for commonality in the language of texting and instant messaging. Our research led us to a necessary expansion of Jeff's brainchild.

"AMASSED" here, is what we believe to be an insightful reference of the generally accepted, most popular, and frequently used **A**cronyms, **M**etaphors, **A**bbreviations, **S**imilies, **S**ymbols, **E**ncryptions, and **D**o-fers.

Some of our listings are pretty raw or insulting, as you will see. We are sorry if anyone is offended by some of these, however, they are the ones that we feel are most necessary to be aware of, and therefore must be included. We have young grandchildren, so being politically correct here would be irresponsible and counterproductive for all of us. We personally felt, with the ongoing, rampant misuse of the internet by unsavory characters and dangerous predators, that by flagging "dangerous entries" we would have a way for parents to recognize distasteful or possibly harmful text if it were to appear in their children's messages.

We've had a lot of fun putting this book together but more importantly, we've learned much about the dangers of the internet, which we feel compelled to pass on to our readers. We now understand how to combat these dangers by applying what we've learned to make our own online experiences safer. We've begun our "thumbers" journey and have progressed from neophyte all the way to advanced-beginner.

We hope that you'll be able to use what we've put forth in this book to bring you and your children closer by safely sharing information and experiences.

Thanks, Jeff, for your inspiration!

The History of "Thumbers[1]"

---

[1] Text-ers and IM-ers. We coined the word "thumbers" because most people use their thumbs for texting. We also included "THMR" in our alphabetical "AMASSED" listing, because we thought it was cool, and, because we could!

The earliest thumbers thumbed a telegraph key, which was the earliest keyboard. They thumbed Morse-Code, which was the original text message. Then there was a long texting drought; until the advent of the personal pager.

07734…This was the first texting we ever did…and that was on a pager! We thought we were so clever with our upside down 'hELLO'. The early pagers only had numbers, so you were really limited with the messages you could send; 911 if you needed a fast reply, 411 for information, asked or given, and a few others. In our household, 1111 meant that our son Jon was home, hopefully before curfew, 2222 alerted us that our daughter Kelley had arrived home safe and sound. A single 1 was for us to call Jon, and a single 2 meant that Kelley needed something. There were a few more numbers that could be used like…143 = I Love You, but no universal language.

The first text message to a cell phone was in the early 1990s, sent from a computer, because at that time cell phones didn't have keyboards. If we correctly recall, the message was "Merry Christmas".

In the late 1990s, keyboards were readily available on cells, and the youth took to SMS (Short Message Service), commonly known as texting. You could communicate in noisy situations, parties, restaurants, sporting events, etc. Students could communicate in school when they weren't allowed to talk. Young lovers could say things to the opposite sex that they didn't have the nerve to say face-to-face. It felt secretive, so it was even more fun!

Today's youth became the fastest thumbs in the West. In fact, young texters the world over are trying hard to beat speed texting records and end up in the Guinness Book of World Records. At the time of this publication, 16-year-old Ang Chuang Yang of Singapore, who texted the required 160 characters in 41:52 seconds, holds the speed record. The official text message is: "The razor-toothed piranhas of the genera Serrasalmus and Pygocentrus are the most ferocious freshwater fish in the world. In reality they seldom attack a human." Wow, we can hardly read it much less text it!

There was a competition between the SMS texting and telegraph operators as well. The victor in one such contest was 93-year-old Gordon Hill versus a 13-year-old teenager, Brittany Devlin. Even though the teen was able to use texting slang, the 93-year-old Morse-Coded every letter to victory. If you're astonished by speed, how's this for volume? Sacramento teen, Crystal Wiski, texted over 300,000 messages in a 30-day period! Crystal's mom is happy her service has free texting.

Now the corporate crowd has taken notice. People are able to check and affirm facts during meetings without interrupting others. The sales force could barter without fearing face to face "tells", or voice inflections that may be adverse on the phone, possibly causing missed or flawed transactions.

Corporate loves the group texting feature for important messages or meeting changes that need to go out fast and reach many people world-wide. The general population is now gaining interest because they found that, to name just a few, they can:

- Purchase event tickets
- Enter contests
- Check bank balances
- Get weather reports
- Express opinions in polls
- Check air fares
- Send Email
- Play games
- Vote for MVP of their favorite team
- Vote for American Idol, Dancing with the Stars,

...and much, much more!

Our 20-something neighbor, Sarah, a surgical tech, likes to text during down times between surgeries when it would be disruptive to others for her to talk on the phone. Sarah is a self-admitted texting addict who can, and has, texted for several hours straight. There really are many reasons for texting!

Just for fun and for your information, we've included the Morse Code used by one of the previous mentioned contestants, along with the 10-Codes used by Police and Emergency Services, and the Phonetic Alphabet used by military and others. Enjoy!

Flagged Items

We have flagged all entries which may indicate harmful or dangerous situations for minors. As examples:

BYOB...Bring Your Own Bottle...
indicating that there is going to be a get-together or party where drinking will occur.

DAD...Dope All Day...
it's not about anyone's father, but rather about doing drugs all day. You would like to know if your children's friends have acceptable life standards.

MIRL...Meet In Real Life...
this could be an acronym of REAL DANGER as in the case of a pedophile attempting to actually meet with your child.

Knowing **"The Code"** will help inform you about your offspring's attitudes and habits, good and bad.

It will enable you to nip negative influences in the bud and enhance positives. We flag drinking, smoking, the most vulgar words, drug use, sexual items and practices, unhealthy relationship examples, and general and extreme dangers of all kinds.

This is not to say that we want to help to create prying, interfering parents. Rather, we hope to help concerned parents guide their children through a better, safer life. It is impossible to be all-inclusive because what's cool today maybe out tomorrow. Cool keeps reinventing itself. We do however, try to include the most frequently used expressions and to encompass all areas of fad communication.

We are not responsible for any errors or omissions. Please enjoy this book, we hope **"The Code"** will serve you well.

"Smileys"

@:-}	Afro
0:-)	Angel
0;-)	Angel Wink
:-z	Angry
~:o	Baby
#:-(	Bad Hair Day
d:-)	Baseball Capped
:~-(	Bawling
:=	Beaver
:-X	Big Kiss
(:-D	Blabber Mouth
?-(	Black Eye
#-)	Blinking
[:-]	Blockhead
:-!	Bored / Foot in Mouth
:-)X	Bowtie Guy
:-C	Bummed Out / Real Unhappy
}:^#)	Censored
C=:-)	Chef

*<<<<+	Christmas Tree
*<):o)	Clown
%-|	Confused / Up All Night
:'-(	Crying
&:-)	Curly Hair
:-@!	Cursing
>:->	Devilish
;-,	Duh
<:-|	Dunce
?-)	Eyeballing
|:-)	Flattop
@>-;--	Flower
%@:-{	Freaking Out
/:-|	Frenchman
8)	Frog
:-<	Frowning
:-/	Frustrated / Skeptical
X:-)	Girl with Bow
)8-)	Google Eyes

:)	Guy Smiley
:-})	Handlebar Moustache
%-)	Happy Drunk
:^{=	Hippie
(H)	Hug
:-o	Hungry / Singing
#*}	Inebriated
:-x	Kiss
:-D	Laughing
>;->	Lewd Dude
:-9	Licking Lips
:-#	Lips are Sealed / New Braces
8:-)	Little Girl
%+{	Lost the Fight
:-{	Mad
;-(	Mad Look
:-(*)	Makes Me Sick
:-S	Makes No Sense / Gibberish
:-)-^<	Man

=:-)	Mohawk
:-{)	Moustache
:-}	Nervous
:^)	Nosy
:8)	Pig
P-|	Pirate
+<:-)	Pope
:-[	Pouting / Vampire
;~[	Prizefighter
=:)	Punk
=:-(	Punked Out
:-r	Raspberries
~:-(	Really Bummed Out
:-))	Really Happy
[:]	Robot
(:-)	Round Face
3:*>	Rudolph the Red Nosed Reindeer
:-(	Sad
*<|:-)	Santa

:-@	Screaming
8-0	Shocked / Oh My God
:-V	Shouting
:-)	Smiley
:-,	Smirk
;^)	Smirking
~~8}	Snake
:-(- <|	Standing Firm
(-:	Standing on Head
:-0	Surprised / Talkative
`:-|	Sweating
:-S	Talking Gibberish
%-\	Tired
:-&	Tongue Tied
=|:-)	Uncle Sam
X-(	Very Mad
:-7	Very Skeptical
%'|	Very Tired
8-)	Wearing Contacts

B-)	Wearing Glasses
}:-)	Wearing Toupee
[:-)	Wearing Walkman
:-1	Whatever
:-"	Whistling
;^?	Wigged Out
'-)	Winking
#-|	Wiped Out
:-)8-<	Woman
:~)	Wondering
:-(0)	Yelling
$-)	Yuppie

Morse Code

A	. -	di-dah
B	- . . .	dah-di-di-dit
C	- . - .	dah-di-dah-dit
D	- . .	dah-di-dit
E	.	dit
F	. . - .	di-di-dah-dit
G	- - .	dah-dah-dit
H	. . . .	di-di-di-dit
I	. .	di-dit
J	. - - -	di-dah-dah-dah
K	- . -	dah-di-dah
L	. - . .	di-dah-di-dit
M	- -	dah-dah
N	- .	dah-dit
O	- - -	dah-dah-dah
P	. - - .	di-dah-dah-dit
Q	- - . -	dah-dah-di-dah
R	. - .	di-dah-dit
S	. . .	di-di-dit
T	-	dah
U	. . -	di-di-dah
V	. . . -	di-di-di-dah
W	. - -	di-dah-dah
X	- . . -	dah-di-di-dah
Y	- . - -	dah-di-dah-dah
Z	- - . .	dah-dah-di-dit

0	- - - - -	dah-dah-dah-dah-dah
1	. - - - -	di-dah-dah-dah-dah
2	. . - - -	di-di-dah-dah-dah
3	. . . - -	di-di-di-dah-dah
4	. . . . -	di-di-di-di-dah
5	. . . . .	di-di-di-di-dit
6	-	dah-di-di-di-dit
7	- - . . .	dah-dah-di-di-dit
8	- - - . .	dah-dah-dah-di-dit
9	- - - - .	dah-dah-dah-dah-dit

Full stop	. - . - . -	di-dah-di-dah-di-dah
Comma	- - . . - -	dah-dah-di-di-dah-dah
Semi-colon	- . - . - .	dah-di-dah-di-dah-dit
Hyphen	- . . . . -	dah-di-di-di-di-dah
Question Mark	. . - - . .	di-di-dah-dah-di-dit
Invitation to Transmit	- . -	dah-di-dah
Wait	. - . . .	di-dah-di-di-dit
End of Message	. - . - .	dah-di-dah-di-dah-dit
End of Work	. . . - . -	di-di-di-dah-di-dah

Error	. . . .	di-di-di-di-di-di-di-dit
Received Message	. - .	di-dah-dit
Separation	- . . . -	dah-di-di-di-dah

10-CODES
Used by Public Safety and Communications People

As you review our composite "10-Codes" list, it will become self-evident that a major problem exists. It should be noted that in some arenas, "11-Codes", "900 Series Codes", "Code-1 Series", and others are also used. There is a lack of uniformity. We are only writers and have no enforcement powers, but we do plead for a national/international uniform set of "10-Codes", for safety's sake. If you, any of our readers, have the ability and wherewithal, to correct this dangerous practice, please do so, on behalf of all of us.

10-00	Officer Down-All Respond
10-0	Caution / Death
10-1	Cannot Understand Message / Officer Needs Help / Call Command
10-2	Reception is Good
10-3	Stop Transmitting / Channel Emergency
10-4	Message Received / Affirmative
10-5	Relay Information to ____ / Repeat
10-6	Station is Busy / Stand By
10-7	Out of Service / Deceased
10-8	In Service
10-9	Repeat Last Message
10-10	Negative / Fight in Progress / Off Duty / Possible Crime
10-11	____ in Service / Dog-Animal Case / Alarm Call / Roadside Check

10-12	Stand By / Stop / Visitors Present / Disregard / At Scene
10-13	Advise Conditions: Weather, Road / Officer Needs Assistance
10-14	Information / Prowler / Citizen Holding Suspect / Check Plate
10-15	Message Delivered / Civil Disturbance / Prisoner in Custody
10-16	Reply to Message / Domestic Disturbance / Vehicle Stolen / Pick Up Prisoner
10-17	Pick Up Papers at ____ / En Route / Meet Complainant / Request Gasoline / Not Stolen
10-18	Urgent / Quickly / Equipment Exchange / Active Warrants
10-19	Contact ____ / Return to ____ / No Warrants
10-20	Unit Location
10-21	Call ____ By Telephone
10-22	Cancel Last Message / Disregard
10-23	Arrived at Scene / Stand By
10-24	Emergency Back Up / Assignment Completed / Request Car to Car Transmission
10-25	Meet ____ / Do You Have Contact With ____
10-26	ETA is ____ / Detaining Subject / Clear
10-27	Request License Check / Moving to Channel
10-28	Request Registration Check
10-29	Check Records For Wanted, Warrants
10-30	Use Caution / Non-conforming Use of Radio / Robbery in Progress

10-31	Pick Up / Crime in Progress
10-32	Radio Check / Person With Gun / Drowning / DWI Test
10-33	Emergency! Officer Needs Help! / Alarm Sounding / Bomb
10-34	Correct Time / Riot / Assist At Office
10-35	Time Check / Major Crime Alert / Confidential Information
10-36	Correct Time of Day
10-37	Suspicious Vehicle / Identify Yourself / Wrecker Needed At _____
10-38	Stopping Suspicious Vehicle / Traffic Stop / Road Block / Message Delivered / Backing Up
10-39	Urgent-Use Lights and Siren / Can _____ Come to the Radio?
10-40	Silent-No Lights or Siren / Is _____ Available for a Phone Call? / Shots Fired
10-41	Beginning Duty / Radio Test
10-42	Ending Duty / Check on Welfare Of _____ At _____ / Traffic Accident At _____
10-43	Information / Call A Doctor / Traffic Jam At _____
10-44	Permission To Leave Duty / Message For You / HazMat Condition
10-45	Driver's License Warrant Check / Fatality / Pick Up Officer / Condition of Patient / Animal Carcass At _____
10-46	Assist Motorist / Ambulance En Route

10-47	Missing Person / Emergency Road Repairs At ____ / Drunk Driver
10-48	Traffic Control At ____ / Runaway Juvenile
10-49	Traffic Light Repair At ____ / Proceed to ____ / Emergency-Clear Air
10-50	Accident (Fatal, Personal Injury, Property Damage) / Under Drug Influence / Take a Report / Officer Welfare Check / Traffic Stop / No-Negative
10-51	Wrecker Needed / Subject is Drunk / Wandering Gang Activity
10-52	Ambulance Needed / Accident With Injuries
10-53	Road Blocked At ____ / Person Down
10-54	Fatal Accident / Negative / Animals On Highway
10-55	Coroner's Case / Suspected DUI / Safety Check & Random Stop (*Which is Unconstitutional, BTW*)
10-56	Intoxicated Driver or Pedestrian / Suicide
10-57	Hit and Run / Firearm Discharged / Intoxicated Person
10-58	Direct Traffic / Garbage Complaint
10-59	Convoy or Escort / Security Check / Bomb Threat
10-60	Squad in Vicinity / Lock Out / Traffic Stop
10-61	Isolate Self for Message / Public Service / Subject Has Record, No Wants
10-62	Reply to Message / Meet A Citizen / Subject

10-63	Possibly Wanted / Unable to Copy-Use Phone Prepare to Make Written Copy / Subject Positive
10-64	Message for Local Delivery / Found Property
10-65	Net Message Assignment / Missing Person / Prepare to Copy / Kidnapping
10-66	Message Cancellation / Suspicious Person / Check Officer Well Being
10-67	Clear for Net Message / Person Calling for Help / Subject is Parolee / All Units Comply
10-68	Dispatch Information / Call for Police Via Phone
10-69	Message Received / Dangerous Subject / Sniper
10-70	Fire / Fire Alarm / Prowler
10-71	Advise Nature of Fire / Shooting / Lewd or Sexual Act
10-72	Report Progress on Fire / Knifing / DOA
10-73	Smoke Report / Receive OK?
10-74	Negative
10-75	In Contact With ____
10-76	En Route ____
10-77	ETA / High Jacking / Situation Under Control
10-78	Need Assistance
10-79	Notify Coroner / Bomb Threat / Hit and Run
10-80	Chase in Progress / Explosion / Armed and Dangerous
10-81	Breathalyzer / Burglar Alarm / Traffic Stop Initiated

10-82	Reserve Lodging / Traffic Signal Out / Stop for Interrogation-Arrest
10-83	Work School Crossing at ____ / Call Station
10-84	Advise ETA / My Telephone # is ____
10-85	Delayed Due To ____ / Prepare to Copy Info
10-86	Officer On Duty / Any Messages For Me
10-87	Pick Up Checks / Meet Officer at ____ / Prisoner Pick Up or Transfer
10-88	Advise Telephone Number / Assume Your Post
10-89	Yes / Bomb Threat
10-90	Bank Alarm at ____ / Alarm Going Off at ____
10-91	Pick Up Prisoner-Subject / Animal Call / Gas Up
10-92	Improperly Parked Vehicle / Your Signal is Weak
10-93	Blockade / Check My Frequency
10-94	Drag Racing / Change to Channel ____
10-95	Prisoner-Subject in Custody / Pedestrian / Request Tech Unit / Officer's Residence
10-96	Mental Subject / Out Of Vehicle-Send Back Up / Detain Prisoner-Subject
10-97	Text Signal / At Scene / Record Information
10-98	Prison-Jail Break / Available for Assignment / Criminal History Indicated

10-99	Wanted-Stolen Indicated / Cardiac Arrest-Death / Officer Needs Assistance / Restroom Quest
10-100	Misdemeanor Warrant / Dead Body / Hot Pursuit/ Riot Conditions Exist / Controlled Substance/ Starting Security Check / Supervisor
10-101	Ending Security Check
10-105	DOA
10-108	Officer Down / Officer In Danger
10-109	Suicide
10-110	Juvenile Disturbance
10-200	Police Needed / Narcotics-Drugs Involved / Restroom Break
10-1000	Felony Warrant / Dead Person
10-2000	Police Required Immediately

Although there are some variations, this is the most uniform list we could develop. Many lesser used entries are not included.

Phonetic Alphabet

Letter	Phonetic Equivalent(s)		
A	Alpha	Adam	
B	Bravo	Baker	Boston
	Boy		
C	Charlie	Cocoa	Charles
D	Delta	David	
E	Echo	Edward	
F	Fox	Foxtrot	Frank
G	Golf	George	
H	Hotel	Henry	
I	India	Ida	
J	Juliett	John	
K	Kilo	King	
L	Lima	Lincoln	
M	Mike	Mary	
N	November	Nora	
O	Oscar	Ocean	
P	Papa	Paul	
Q	Quebec	Queen	
R	Romeo	Robert	
S	Sierra	Sam	
T	Tango	Tom	
U	Uniform	Union	
V	Victor	Victor	

Letter	Phonetic Equivalent(s)	
W	Whiskey	William
X	X-ray	X-ray
Y	Yankee	Young
Z	Zulu	Zebra

"Amassed"

	1	Won
	2	To / Too / Peace
	4	For
	5	Gimme Five
	6	I'm Busy
	7	I'm Leaving
🚩	8	Oral Sex
🚩	9	Parent is watching
🚩	12	Someone Present
🚩	16	Meet At
	17	Urgent
	19	Zero (-0-) Hand
	20	Location
	21	Call Me
🚩	22	Meet
	36	Time
🚩	81	Hell's Angels
	86	Eliminate It
	88	Goodbye
🚩	99	Parent is no longer watching
🚩	121	One To One = Private Chat

🚩	143	I Love You
🚩	182	I Hate You
	404	Don't Know
	411	Information
🚩	420	Toke Time / Marijuana
🚩	459	I Love You
	555	Cry. *(More 5s = more intense)*
🚩	831	I Love You
🚩	1174	Nude Club
🚩	1337	"leet" / Elite
	!	I have a comment
	*VIN	Starvin'
	;S	Confused
	?	Question / don't understand
	?4U	Question for you
	@TEOTD	At The End Of The Day
	\M/	Heavy Metal Music
	^5	High Five
	^RUP^	Read Up Please
	^URS	Up Yours
🚩	<3	"Heart" - Love, Pal, Buddy *(More 3s = more intense)*

10-4	OK / Good Bye
14AAA41	One for All And All for One
1DR	Wonder
2B/-2B	To Be Or Not To Be
2BZ4U	Too Busy For You
2G2B4GTN	Too Good To Be Forgotten
2G2BT	Too Good To Be True
2MI	Too Much Information
2MRO	Tomorrow
2NITE	Tonight
2U2	To You Too
4COL	For Crying Out Loud
4EAE	Forever and Ever
🚩 4F	Find em, feel em, f**k em, forget em
4FR	Forever
4FRNFR	Forever and Ever
4NR	Foreigner
🚩 4Q	F**k You
4VR	Forever
4VRNVR	Forever and Ever

🚩	5FS	Five Finger Salute = Jerk Off or Male Masturbation
🚩	5-O	Police
🚩	6Y	Sexy
🚩	A/S/L/P	Age, Sex, Location, Picture
🚩	A3	Anytime, Any place, Any where
	AA	As Above
	AAAAA	American Association Against Acronym Abuse
	AAF	As A Friend
	AAK	Asleep At Keyboard
	AAMOF	As A Matter Of Fact
	AAMOI	As A Matter Of Interest
	AAP	Always A Pleasure
	AAR	At Any Rate
	AAR8	At Any Rate
	AAS	Alive And Smiling
	AATK	Always At The Keyboard
	AAYF	As Always, Your Friend
	AB	Ass Backwards
	ABITH	A Bird In The Hand
	ABITHIW-2ITB	A Bird In The Hand Is Worth Two In The Bush

🚩	A-BOOT	Under influence of drugs
	ABT	About
	ABT2	About to
	ACD	Alt Control Delete
	ACE	Access Control Entry
	ACK	Acknowledgement
	ACORN	A Completely Obsessive Really Nutty Person
	ADAD	Another Day Another Dollar
	ADBB	All Done Bye Bye
🚩	ADD	Address
	ADIH	Another Day In Hell
	ADIP	Another Day In Paradise
	ADN	Any Day Now / Advanced Digital Network
🚩	ADR	Address
	AEAP	As Early As Possible
	AFAGAU	A Friend As Good As You
	AFAGAY	A Friend As Good As You
	AFAHM-ASP	A Fool And His Money Are Soon Parted
	AFAIA	As Far As I'm Aware
	AFAIC	As Far As I'm Concerned

AFAICS	As Far As I Can See	
AFAICT	As Far As I Can Tell	
AFAIK	As Far As I Know	
AFAIR	As Far As I Remember	
AFAIU	As Far As I Understand	
AFAIUI	As Far As I Understand It	
AFAP	As Far As Possible	
AFAYC	As Far As You're Concerned	
AFC	Away From Computer	
🚩 AFDN	Any F**king Day Now	
🚩 AFGO	Another F**king Growth Opportunity	
AFINIAFI	A Friend In Need Is A Friend Indeed	
AFJ	April Fool's Joke	
AFK	Away From Keyboard / A Free Kill	
AFPOE	A Fresh Pair Of Eyes	
🚩 AFT	About F**king Time	
AFZ	Acronym Free Zone	
AGB	Almost Good Bridge	
AGKWE	And God Knows What Else	
AH	At Home	

AIAMU	And I'm A Monkey's Uncle
AIGHT	All Right
AIH	As It Happens
AIMB	As I Mentioned Before
AIMP	Always In My Prayers
AIR	As I Remember
AISB	As I Said Before / As It Should Be
AISE	As I Said Earlier
AISI	As I See It
🚩 AITR	Adult In The Room
AKA	Also Known As
ALAP	As Late As Possible
ALCON	All Concerned
ALOL	Actually Laughing Out Loud
ALOTBSOL	Always Look On The Bright Side Of Life
ALTG	Act Locally, Think Globally
AMAP	As Much As Possible
AMBW	All My Best Wishes
🚩 AMF	Adios Mother F**ker
🚩 AMFM	Adios Mother F**king Moron

AML	All My Love
AMPG	Above My Pay Grade
🚩 AMRMTY-FTS	All My Roommates Thank You For The Show
ANAWFOS	And Now A Word From Our Sponsors
ANFSCD	And Now For Something Completely Different
ANGB	Almost Nearly Good Bridge
🚩 ANLOC	Analoculitis
AOAS	All Of A Sudden
AOB	Abuse Of Bandwidth
🚩 AOM	Age Of Majority
AON	Apropos Of Nothing
AOTA	All Of The Above
AOYP	Angel On Your Pillow
AOYS	Angel On Your Shoulder
AP	Apple Pie
APAC	All Praise And Credit
AQAP	As Quick As Possible / As Quiet As Possible
ART	All Right
AS	Ape Shit / Another Subject
🚩 ASAFP	As Soon As F**king Possible

| 51

ASAP	As Soon As Possible
ASAYGT	As Soon As You Get This
🚩 ASL	Age, Sex, Location
🚩 ASLA	Age, Sex, Location, Availability
🚩 ASLMH	Age, Sex, Location, Music, Hobbies
AT	At Your Terminal
ATAB	Ain't That A Bitch
ATC	Any Two Cards
ATEOD	At The End Of The Day
ATM	At The Moment
ATSITS	All The Stars In The Sky
ATSL	Along The Same Line(s)
ATST	At The Same Time
🚩 ATW	Around The Web / All The Way
AW	At Work
AWC	After While, Crocodile
AWGTHT-GTTA	Are We Going To Have to Go Through This Again
AWHFY	Are We Having Fun Yet
AWLTP	Avoiding Work Like The Plague
AWNIAC	All We Need Is Another Chair

🚩 AWOL	Absent Without Leave / Absent Without Official Leave
AWTTW	A Word To The Wise
AYC	Aren't You Clever / Aren't You Cheeky
AYCE	All You Can Eat
AYDY	Are You Done Yet
AYEC	At Your Earliest Convenience
AYK	As You Know
AYOR	At Your Own Risk
🚩 AYPF	Adios You Pussy Face
AYS	Are You Serious
AYSOS	Are You Stupid Or Something
AYT	Are You There
AYTMTB	And You're Telling Me This Because
AYV	Are You Vertical
AZN	Asian
B	Back
B&F	Back And Forth
B/C	Because
B4	Before
B4N	Bye For Now

B4U	Before You
B4YKI	Before You Know It
🚩 B8	(Jail) Bait
🚩 BAC	Bad Ass Chick
BAG	Busting A Gut / Big Ass Gun
BAK	Back At Keyboard
🚩 BAMF	Bad Ass Mother F**ker
🚩 BAMFIC	Bad Ass Mother F**ker In Charge
🚩 banana	Penis
BAS	Big Ass Smile
BAU	Business As Usual
BAY	Back At Ya
BB	Be Back
🚩 BB	BeerBoarding
🚩 BBAMFIC	Big Bad Ass Mother F**ker In Charge
BBB	Bye Bye Babe / Boring Beyond Belief
BBBG	Bye Bye Be Good
BBC	Big Bad Challenge
BBFBBM	Body By Fisher, Brains By Mattel
BBFN	Bye Bye For Now

BBIAB	Be Back In A Bit
BBIAF	Be Back In A Few / Be Back In A Flash
BBIAM	Be Back In A Minute
BBIAS	Be Back In A Second
BBIAW	Be Back In A While
BBL	Be Back Later
⚑ BBMFIC	Big Bad Mother F**ker In Charge
BBN	Bye Bye Now
BBQ	BarBeCue
BBR	Burnt Beyond Repair / Burnt Beyond Recognition
BBS	Be Back Soon / Bulletin Board Service
BBSL	Be Back Sooner or Later
BBT	Be Back Tomorrow
BBW	Big Beautiful Woman
BC	Be Cool
BCBG	Bon Chic, Bon Genre
BCBS	Big Company, Big School
BCNU	Be Seeing You
BCUZ	Because

	BD	Big Deal / Brain Drain / Birthday / Brain Damage
	BDAY	Birthday
	BDBI5M	Busy Daydreaming, Back In Five Minutes
	BDC	Big Dumb Company / Big Dot-Com
	BDN	Big Damn Number
	BEG	Big Evil Grin
🚩	BF	Boyfriend / Best Friends
	BF4FR	Best Friends Forever
	BFAW	Best Friend At Work
	BFB	Bad FaceBook / Bogus FaceBook
🚩	BFD	Big F**king Deal
🚩	BFE	Bum F**k Egypt
	BFF	Best Friends Forever
	BFFL	Best Friends For Life
	BFFN	Best Friends For Now
	BFFTTE	Best Friends Forever Til The End
🚩	BFG	Big F**king Grin
	BFO	Blinding Flash of Obvious
	BFN	Bye For Now

🚩	BFR	Big F**king Rock
	BG	Background
	BG	Big Grin
🚩	BGWM	Be Gentle With Me
	BHG	Big Hearted Guy / Big Hearted Girl
	BHL8	Be Home Late
	BHOF	Bald Headed Old Fart
	BI5	Back In Five
	BIAF	Back In A Flash
	BIB	Boss In Back
	BIBI	Bye Bye
🚩	BIBO	Beer In, Beer Out
	BIF	Before I Forget
	BIL	Brother-In-Law
🚩	BIOIYA	Break It Off In Your Ass
	BION	Believe It Or Not
🚩	BIOYA	Blow It Out Your Ass
	BIOYIOP	Blow It Out Your I/O Port
	BIOYN	Blow It Out Your Nose
	BITCH	Basically In The Clear, Homey
	BITD	Back In The Day

🚩	BITFOB	Bring It The F**k On Bitch
🚩	BJ	Blow Job
	BK	Back
	BKA	Better Known As
	BL	Belly Laugh
	BLBBLB	Back Like Bull, Brain Like Bird
	BLNT	Better Luck Next Time
🚩	BM	Byte Me / Bite Me / Bro Mama
	BM&Y	Between Me And You
🚩	BMF	Bad Mother F**ker
	BMGWL	Busting My Gut With Laughter
🚩	BMOF	Bite Me Old Fart
🚩	BMOTA	Bite Me On The Ass
🚩	BNB	Bed n Barf
	BNDN	Been Nowhere, Done Nothing
	BNF	Big Name Fan
🚩	BO	Body Odor / Bug Off / Buzz Off / Burn Out
🚩	BOB	Battery-Operated Boyfriend
	BOBFOC	Body Off Baywatch, Face Off Crime watch
	BOCTAAE	But Of Course There Are Always Exceptions

BOFH	Bastard Operator From Hell
🚩 BOHICA	Bend Over, Here It Comes Again
BOL	Best Of Luck
BOLO	Be On The Lookout
BOME	Based On My Experience
BON	Believe It Or Not
BOOMS	Bored Out Of My Skull
BOTEC	Back Of The Envelope Calculation
BOTOH	But On The Other Hand
🚩 BP	Binge & Purge
BPLM	Big Person, Little Mind
BR	Bathroom
BRB	Be Right Back
BRD	Bored
BRT	Be Right There
BS	Big Smile / Bull Shit / Brain Strain
BSAAW	Big Smile And A Wink
BSBD&-NE	Book Smart, Brain Dead And No Experience
BSEG	Big Shit-Eating Grin
BSF	But Seriously Folks

BSOD	Blue Screen Of Death
BT	Byte This
BTA	But Then Again
BTDT	Been There, Done That
BTDTGTTS	Been There, Done That, Got The T-Shirt
🚩 BTFO	Back The F**k Off / Bend The F**k Over
BTHOOM	Beats The Heck Out Of Me
BTN	Better Than Nothing
🚩 BTS	Break The Seal (first pee when drinking)
BTSOOM	Beats The Shit Out Of Me
BTTT	Back To The Top
BTW	By The Way
BTWBO	Be There With Bells On
🚩 BTWITI-ILWY	By The Way, I Think I'm In Love With You
🚩 BVR	Beaver (vagina)
BW	Best Wishes
BWDIK	But What Do I Know
BWL	Bursting With Laughter
BWO	Black, White or Other
BY&M	Between You And Me

	BYKT	But You Knew That
🚩	BYOA	Bring Your Own Advil
🚩	BYOB	Bring Your Own Bottle / Booze / Beer
🚩	BYOB	Bring Your Own Bitch / Biotch
	BYOC	Bring Your Own Computer
🚩	BYOW	Build Your Own Website / Bring Your Own Wine
	BYTM	Better You Than Me
	BZ	Busy
	C	Cookie
🚩	C&C	Champagne And Cocaine
🚩	C&D	Cease And Desist / Crackheads & Degenerates
	C&E	Christmas And Easter (church goers) / Craps And Eleven
	C&G	Chuckle And Grin
	C&P	Cut And Paste/ Copy And Paste
🚩	C&S	Chew And Spit (weight loss)
	C/P	Cross Point
🚩	C187	Kill, Death
🚩	C4N	plastique explosive
	C4N	Ciao For Now

| 61

	CAAC	Cool As A Cucumber
🚩	CAB	C**t Ass Bitch
	CAS	Crack A Smile
	CB	Coffee Break / Chat Break / Crazy Biotch / Cyber Bully
	CBB	Can't Be Bothered
🚩	CBF	Can't Be F**ked
🚩	CBJ	Covered Blow Job
🚩	CBS	Cyber Sex
🚩	C-C	Condom
🚩	CD9	Code 9 = parents are around
🚩	CE	Casual Encounters
	CF	Coffee Freak
🚩	CFLU	Cocaine Flu (hangover)
	CFN	Ciao For Now
	CFV	Call For a Vote
	CHA	Click Here Asshole
	CIAO	Hello / Goodbye (Italian)
	CICO	Coffee In, Coffee Out
🚩	CICYHW	Can I Copy Your Homework
	CID	Consider It Done / Crying In Disgrace

CIS	CompuServe Information Service
CLAB	Crying Like A Baby
CLM	Career Limiting Move
CM	Call Me
CMA	Cover My Ass
CMAP	Cover My Ass Partner
CMF	Count My Fingers
⚑ CMFB	See My FaceBook / Check out My FaceBook
CMIIW	Correct Me If I'm Wrong
CMON	Come On
⚑ CMOP	See Me On Plaxo
CMU	Crack Me Up
⚑ CMS	See MySpace / Check out MySpace
C'N	Chillin'
CNP	Continued in Next Post
COB	Close Of Business
COD	Change Of Dressing
Cof$	Church of Scientology
CofS	Church of Scientology
COS	Change of Subject / Because

	CP	Cross Post, Go to IM
	CP	Sleepy
	CR8	Create
🚩	CRAFT	Can't Remember A F**king Thing
	CRAP	Cheap Redundant Assorted Products
	CRAT	Can't Remember A Thing
	CRAWS	Can't Remember Anything Worth a Shit
	CRB	Come Right Back
	CRBT	Crying Real Big Tears
	CRDTCK	Credit Check
	CRS	Can't Remember Shit
	CS	Change of Subject
	CS	Career Suicide
	CSA	Cool, Sweet, Awesome
	CSG	Chuckle, Snicker, Grin
	CSL	Can't Stop Laughing
	CT	Can't Talk
	C-T	City
🚩	CTA	Call To Action

🚩	CTC	Choking The Chicken / Care To Chat
🚩	CTFU	Cracking The F**k Up
	CTO	Check This Out
	CU	See You / Cracking Up
	CU2	See You Too
	CUA	See You Around
	CUATU	See You Around The Universe
	CUL	See You Later
	CUL8R	See You Later
	CULA	See You Later Alligator
	CUNS	See You In School
	CUO	See You Around
	CUOL	See You Online
	CUWTA	Catch Up With The Acronyms
	CUZ	Because
	CWOT	Complete Waste Of Time
	CWYL	Chat With You Later
	CX	Cancelled
	CY	Calm Yourself
	CYA	Cover Your Ass / See Ya

CYAL8R	See Ya Later
CYE	Check Your Email
CYEP	Close Your Eyes Partner
CYL	See You Later
CYM	Check Your Mail
CYO	See You Online
CYOA	Cover Your Own Ass
CYT	See You Tomorrow
🚩 D&D	Drug And Disease / Dine And Dash / Dungeons And Dragons
D&M	Deep And Meaningful
🚩 D4D	Down For Dick
🚩 DA	Do Anything / District Attorney
🚩 DAD	Dope All Day
DAMHIKT	Don't Ask Me How I Know That
🚩 DARE	Police Anti-Drug+Alcohol / Drugs Are Really Expensive
DARFC	Ducking And Running For Cover
DB	Douche Bag
DBA	Doing Business As
DBABAI	Don't Be A Bitch About It
DBAU	Doing Business As Usual

DBD	Don't Be Dumb
DBEYR	Don't Believe Everything You Read
DBT	Dumped By Text
DD	Due Diligence / Dear Daughter
DDD	Direct Distance Dial
d-dd	moronic person
DDSOS	Different Day, Same Old Shit
DDSS	Different Day, Same Shit
def	Definitely
DETI	Don't Even Think It
DF	Dear Friend
🚩 DFGT	Don't F**king Go There
DFY	Don't Flatter Yourself
DGA	Don't Go Anywhere
🚩 DGAF	Don't Give A F**k
DGT	Don't Go There
DGTG	Don't Go There, Girlfriend
DGYF	Damn Girl, You're Fine
DH	Dear Husband
DHYB	Don't Hold Your Breath
DIAF	Die In A Fire

🚩	DIC	Drunk In Charge
	DIIK	Damned If I Know
	DIKU	Do I Know You
	DILLIGAD	Does It Look Like I Give A Damn
🚩	DILLIGAF	Does It Look Like I Give A F**k
	DILLIGAS	Does It Look Like I Give A Shit
	DINK	Double Income, No Kids
	DIRFT	Do It Right the First Time
	DIS	Did I Say
	DISTOL	Did I Say That Out Loud
	DITR	Dancing In The Rain
🚩	DITYID	Did I Tell You I'm Distressed
	DIY	Do It Yourself
	DKDC	Don't Know Don't Care
	DL	Download / Dead Link / Down Low
	DLTBBB	Don't Let The Bed Bugs Bite
	DLTM	Don't Lie To Me
	DM	Doesn't Matter
	DMI	Don't Mention It
	DN	Down

DNBL8	Do Not Be Late	
DNC	Does Not Compute	
DND	Do Not Disturb	
🚩 DNE	Drunk And Emotional	
🚩 DNP	Drunk In Public	
🚩 DOC	Drug Of Choice	
DOE	Depends On Everything	
d'oh	A Simpson's Expression (foolery)	
dOOd	Dude	
DORD	Department Of Redundancy Department	
DP	Domestic Partner / Display Picture	
dps	Damage Per Second	
DPUP	Don't Poop Your Pants	
DQMOT	Don't Quote Me On This	
DQYDT	Don't Quit Your Day Job	
DRIB	Don't Read If Busy	
DS	Dear Son	
DSTR8	Damn Straight	
DTC	Deep Throaty Chuckle	
DTRT	Do The Right Thing	

	DTS	Don't Think So
	DUAA	Don't Use Any Acronyms
🚩	DUI	Driving Under the Influence
🚩	DUM	Do You Masturbate
	DUNA	Don't Use No Acronyms
	DUPE	Duplicate
🚩	DURS	Damn You are Sexy
🚩	DUSL	Do You Scream Loud
	DUST	Did You See That
🚩	DV	Designer Vaginer
🚩	DV8	Deviate
	DW	Dear Wife
	DWB	Don't Write Back / Driving While Black
	DWBH	Don't Worry Be Happy
	DWF	Divorced White Female
	DWH2GTTA	Do We Have To Go Through This Again
🚩	DWI	Driving While Intoxicated
	DWM	Divorced White Male
🚩	DWPK-OTL	Deep Wet Passionate Kiss On The Lips
	DWS	Driving While Stupid

🚩 DWT	Driving While Texting
🚩 DWWW-WI	Surfing the World-Wide Web While Intoxicated
D'YA	Do You
DYFM	Dude You Fascinate Me
🚩 DYHAB	Do You Have A Boyfriend
🚩 DYHAG	Do You Have A Girlfriend
DYJHIW	Don't You Just Hate It When...
DYLTHWYH	Did You Leave The House Without Your Helmet
🚩 DYOFDW	Do Your Own F**king Dirty Work
DYOR	Do Your Own Research
🚩 DYSTSOTT	Did You See The Size Of That Thing
DYT	Do You Twitter / Do You Tweet
🚩 E	Ecstasy
E1	Every One
E123	Easy as One, Two, Three
E4T	Effort
EAK	Eating At Keyboard
EBKAC	Error Between Keyboard And Chair
🚩 ED	Erase Display / Erectile Dysfunction

EE	Electronic Emission
🚩 effin	F**king
EFT	Electronic Funds Transfer
EG	Evil Grin
EIP	Editing In Progress
EL	Evil Laugh
EM	Excuse Me
EMA	Email Address
EMFBI	Excuse Me For Butting In
EMI	Excuse My Ignorance
EML	Email Me Later
EMRTW	Evil Monkeys Rule The World
EMSG	Email Message
ENUF	Enough
EOD	End Of the Day
🚩 EOL	End Of Life
EOM	End Of Message
EOT	End Of Thread
ES	Erase Screen
ESAD	Eat Shit And Die
🚩 ESADYFA	Eat Shit And Die You F**king Asshole

ESEMED	Every Second, Every Minute, Every Day	
ESH	Experience, Strength and Hope	
🚩 ESMF	Eat Shit Mother F**ker	
ESO	Equipment Smarter than Operator	
ETA	Estimated Time of Arrival / Edited To Add	
EVA	Ever	
EVO	Evolution	
EVRE1	Every One	
🚩 EWI	Emailing While Intoxicated	
🚩 EZ	Easy	
F2F	Face To Face	
F2P	Free To Play	
F	Female	
🚩 FA	F**king A	
FAB	Features Attributes Benefits	
🚩 FAW-OMFT	Frequently Argued Waste Of My F**king Time	
🚩 FAP	F**king A Pissed	
FAQ	Frequently Asked Questions	
FASB	Fast Ass Som Bitch	
FAWC	For Anyone Who Cares	

🚩	FB	FaceBook
🚩	FB	F**k Buddy
	FBF	Fat Boy Food
🚩	FBI	F**king Brilliant Idea / Female Body Inspector
	FBKS	Failure Between Keyboard and Seat
	FBM	Fine By Me
	FC	Fingers Crossed
	FCFS	First Come, First Served
	FDGB	Fall Down Go Boom
	FE	Fatal Error
	FF	Friends Forever
	FF&PN	Fresh Fields And Pastures New
🚩	FFS	For F**k Sake
	FGDAI	Fuhgedaboudit = Forget About It
	FIC	Farticles (flatulent particulate)
	FICCL	Frankly I Couldn't Care Less
🚩	FIF	F**k I'm Funny
🚩	FIIK	F**k If I Know
	FIIOOH	Forget It I'm Out Of Here
	FIL	Father In Law

🚩	FILF	Father I'd Like to F**k
	FILTH	Failed In London, Try Hong Kong
	FIMH	Forever In My Heart
🚩	FINE	F**ked-up, Insecure, Neurotic, Emotional
	FISH	First In, Still Here
	FITB	Fill In The Blanks
	FMI	For My Information
🚩	FMLTWIA	F**k Me Like The Whore I Am
	FMTYEWTK	Far More Than You Ever Wanted To Know
🚩	FMUTA	F**k Me Up The Ass
🚩	FO	F**k Off
🚩	FOAD	F**k Off And Die
	FOAF	Friend Of A Friend
	FOB	Free On Board
🚩	FOAG	F**k Off And Google
	FOC	Free Of Charge
	FOFL	Falling On Floor Laughing
🚩	FOL	Fond Of Leather
	FOMC	Fell Off My Chair
	FOMCL	Falling Off My Chair Laughing

	FORD	Found On Road Dead / Fix Or Repair Daily
	ForM	Female or Male
	FOS	Full Of Shit
🚩	FRED	F**king Ridiculous Electronic Device
	FS	For Sale
	FSBO	For Sale By Owner
	FSR	For Some Reason
🚩	FSU	F**ing Shut Up
	FTASB	Faster Than A Speeding Bullet
	FTBOMH	From The Bottom Of My Heart
🚩	FTF	Face To Face / F**k That's Funny
🚩	FTFOI	For The Fun Of It / For The F**k Of It
	FTL	Faster Than Light
	FTLOG	For The Love Of God
🚩	FTN	F**k That Noise
	FTR	For The Record
🚩	FTRF	F**k That's Really Funny
	FTTB	For The Time Being
🚩	FTW	For The Win / F**k The World

🚩	FU2	F**k You Too
🚩	FUBAR	F**ked Up Beyond All Recognition
🚩	FUBB	F**ked Up Beyond Belief
	FUD	Fear, Uncertainty, Disinformation
🚩	FUJIMO	F**k You Jack I'm Movin' On
🚩	FUM	F**ked Up Mess
	FURTB	Filled Up and Ready To Burst
🚩	FWB	Friends With Benefits
	FWD	Forward
	FWIW	For What It's Worth
	FYA	For Your Amusement
	FYE	For Your Edification
🚩	FYEO	For Your Eyes Only
	FYF	From Your Friend
	FYI	For Your Information
🚩	FYIFV	F**k You I'm Fully Vested
	FYLTGE	From Your Lips To God's Ear
	FYM	For Your Misinformation
🚩	FYSBI-GBABN	Fasten Your Seat Belts, It's Gonna Be A Bumpy Night
	G	Guess / Grin / Giggle
	G1	Good One

G2CU	Good To See You
G2G	Got To Go
G2GLYS	Got To Go, Love You So
G2R	Got To Run
GA	Go Ahead
🚩 GAB	Getting A Beer
🚩 GAB	Getting Another Beer
GAL	Get A Life
🚩 GALGAL	Give A Little, Get A Little
GALHER	Get A Load of Her
GALHIM	Get A Load of Him
🚩 GAP	Got A Pic / Gay Ass People
GAS	Got A Second
GB	Good Bridge / Good Bye
GBG	Great Big Grin
GBH	Great Big Hug
GBU	God Bless You
GBY	God Bless You
GC	Good Crib
GD&R	Grinning, Ducking And Running
GD&RF	Grinning, Ducking And Running Fast

🚩 GDI	God Damn It / God Damn Independent
GDW	Grin, Duck and Wave
GF	Girlfriend
🚩 GFF	Go F**king Figure
GFI	Go For It
GFN	Gone For Now
🚩 GFON	Good For One Night
GFR	Grim File Reaper
GFTD	Gone For The Day
🚩 GFY	Good For You / Go F**k Yourself
🚩 GFYMF	Go F**k Yourself Mother F**ker
GG	Good Game / Gotta Go
GGA	Good Game All
GGN	Gotta Go Now
GGOH	Gotta Get Out of Here
GGP	Gotta Go Pee
GH	Good Hand
GI	Google It
GIAR	Give It A Rest
🚩 GIC	Gift In Crib

GIDK	Gee I Don't Know
GIGO	Garbage In, Garbage Out
🚩 GIRL	Guy In Real Life
GIWIST	Gee, I Wish I'd Said That
GJ	Good Job
GJP	Good Job Partner
GL	Good Luck / Get Lost
GL/HF	Good Luck, Have Fun
GLA	Good Luck All
🚩 GLBT	Gay, Lesbian, Bisexual, Transgender
GLG	Good Looking Girl
GLGH	Gook Luck and Good Hunting
GLYASDI	God Loves You And So Do I
GM	Good Morning / Good Move
GMAB	Give Me A Break
🚩 GMAFB	Give Me A F**king Break
GMAO	Giggling My Ass Off
GMTA	Great Minds Think Alike
GMTFT	Great Minds Think For Themselves
GN	Good Night

🚩	GNBLFY	Got Nothing But Love For You
🚩	GNOC	Get Naked On Cam
	GNSD	Good Night, Sweet Dreams
🚩	GO	Get Off
	GOI	Get Over It
	GOK	God Only Knows
	GOL	Giggling Out Loud
🚩	GOS	Gay Or Straight
	GOWI	Get On With It
	GOYHH	Get Off Your High Horse
	GR&D	Grinning, Running And Ducking
	GR2BR	Good Riddance To Bad Rubbish
	GR8	Great
	GRATZ	Congratulations
	GRL	Girl
	GRRR	Growling
	GRWG	Get Right With God
🚩	GSOAS	Go Sit On A Snake
	GT	Good Try
🚩	GTFO	Get The F**k Out
🚩	GTFOH	Get The F**k Outta Here

🚩	GTFOOH	Get The F**k Out Of Here
	GTG	Got To Go
	GTGB	Got To Go, Bye
	GTGP	Got To Go Pee
	GTH	Go To Hell
	GTHA	Get The Hell Away
	GTK	Good To Know
	GTM	Giggle To Myself
	GTRM	Going To Read Mail
	GTSY	Glad To See You
🚩	GUD	Graphically Undesirable
	GWI	Get With It
	GWS	Get Well Soon
	GYHOOYA	Get Your Head Out Of Your Ass
	GYHOYA	Get Your Head Outta Your Ass
🚩	GYPO	Get Your Pants Off
	H&K	Hugs And Kisses
	H/O	Hold On
	H/P	Hold Please
	H2CUS	Hope To See You Soon
🚩	H4U	Hot For You

🚩	H4XXOR	Hacker / To be hacked
🚩	H8	Hate
	HAGD	Have A Great Day
	HAGN	Have A Good Night
	HAGO	Have A Good One
	HAK	Hugs And Kisses
	HAND	Have A Nice Day
	HAU	How About You
	HAWTLW	Hello And Welcome To Last Week
🚩	HLP	Help
	HB	Hurry Back
	HBASTD	Hitting Bottom And Starting To Dig
	HBB	Hip Beyond Belief
🚩	HBIB	Hot But Inappropriate Boy
	HBU	How 'Bout You
	HCC	Holy Computer Crap
	HF	Have Fun / Have Faith
	HGZ	Hugs
	HHIS	Hanging Head In Shame
	HHO-1/2K	Ha Ha, Only Half Kidding

HHOJ	Ha Ha, Only Joking
HHOK	Ha Ha, Only Kidding
HHOS	Ha Ha, Only Serious
HHTYAY	Happy Holidays To You And Yours
HIG	How's It Going
HIH	Hope It Helps
HIOOC	Help, I'm Out Of Coffee
HIT	Hang In There
HITKS	Hang In There, Keep Smiling
HL	Half Life
HLD	Hold
⚑ HMFIC	Head MoFo In Charge
HNTI	How Nice That Is / This Is
HNTW	How Nice That Was
HNY	Happy New Year
HO	Hold On
HOAS	Hold On A Second
⚑ HOHA	Hollywood Hacker
⚑ HOIC	Hold On, I'm Coming
HOYEW	Hanging On Your Every Word
HP	Higher Power / Hit Points

HPPO	Highest Paid Person in Office
HRU	How Are You
HSIK	How Should I Know
HT	Hi There
HTB	Hang The Bastards
HTH	Hope This Helps
HTNOTH	Hit The Nail On The Head
HUA	Head Up Ass
HUB	Head Up Butt
HUYA	Head Up Your Ass
HV	Have
HWGA	Here We Go Again
🚩 I&I	Intercourse And Inebriation
I1DR	I Wonder
IAC	In Any Case / I Am Confused
IAE	In Any Event
IANAC	I Am Not A Crook
IANAE	I Am Not An Expert
IANAL	I Am Not A Lawyer
IANNN-GC	I Am Not Nurturing the Next Generation of Casualties

	IASAP4U	I Always Say A Prayer For You
	IAT	I Am Tired
	IAW	I Agree With / In Accordance With
🚩	IAYM	I Am Your Master
	IB	I'm Back
	IBGYBG	I'll Be Gone, You'll Be Gone
	IBIWISI	I'll Believe It When I See It
	IBK	Idiot Behind Keyboard
	IBRB	I'll Be Right Back
	IBT	In Between Technology
🚩	IBTC	Itty Bitty Titty Committee
	IBTD	I Beg To Differ
	IBTL	In Before The Lock
	IC	In Character / I See
	ICAM	I Couldn't Agree More
	ICBW	I Could Be Wrong / It Could Be Worse
	ICEDI	I Can't Even Discuss It
	ICYC	In Case You're Curious / In Case You Care
	IDC	I Don't Care
🚩	IDGAF	I Don't Give A F**k

	IDGARA	I Don't Give A Rat's Ass
	IDGI	I Don't Get It / I Don't Get Involved
	IDK	I Don't Know
🚩	IDKU	I Don't Know You
🚩	IDKY	I Don't Know You
	IDL	Ideal
	IDM	It Doesn't Matter
	IDST	I Didn't Say That
	IDTA	I Did That Already
	IDTS	I Don't Think So
	IDUNNO	I Don't Know
🚩	IF/IB	In Front/In Back
	IFAB	I Found A Bug
🚩	IFU	I F**ked Up
	IG2R	I Got To Run
	IGGP	I Gotta Go Pee
🚩	IGHT	I Got High Tonight
	IGN	I've Got Nothing
	IGP	I Gotta Pee
	IGTP	I Get The Point
	IHA	I Hate Acronyms

IHAIM	I Have Another Instant Message
IHNO	I Have No Opinion
🚩 IHTFP	I Have Truly Found Paradise / I Hate This F**king Place
IHU	I Hear You
IIABDFI	If It Ain't Broke, Don't Fix It
IIIO	Intel Inside, Idiot Outside
IIMAD	If It Makes Any Difference
IIR	If I Remember / If I Recall
IIRC	If I Remember Correctly / If I Recall Correctly
🚩 IIT	Is It Tight
IITLYTO	If It's Too Loud You're Too Old
🚩 IITYWYBMAD	If I Tell You Will You Buy Me A Drink
IIWM	If It Were Me
IJPMP	I Just Pissed My Pants
IJWTK	I Just Want To Know
IJWTS	I Just Want To Say
IK	I Know
IKALOPLT	I Know A Lot Of People Like That
IKWYM	I Know What You Mean
IKYABWAI	I Know You Are But What Am I

	ILA	I Love Acronyms
	ILBL8	I'll Be Late
🚩	ILFD	I Love Female Dominance
🚩	ILMD	I Love Male Dominance
	ILQ	I Like You
🚩	ILU	I Love You
	ILUAAF	I Love You As A Friend
	ILUM	I Love You Man
🚩	ILY	I Love You
	IM	Instant Messaging
	IM2BZ2P	I Am Too Busy To Pee
	IMA	I Might Add
	IMAO	In My Arrogant Opinion
	IMCO	In My Considered Opinion
	IME	In My Experience
🚩	IMEZRU	I Am Easy, Are You
	IMHEIUO	In My High Exalted Informed Unassailable Opinion
	IMHO	In My Humble Opinion
	IMNAL	I Am Not A Lawyer
	IMNERHO	In My Never Even Remotely Humble Opinion

IMNSHO	In My Not So Humble Opinion
IMO	In My Opinion
IMOO	In My Own Opinion
IMPOV	In My Point Of View
IMRU	I Am, Are You?
IMS	I Am Sorry
IMSB	I Am So Bored
IMTM	I Am The Man
IMU	I Miss You
INADBIPOOTV	I'm Not A Doctor, But I Play One On TV
INBD	Its No Big Deal
INMP	Its Not My Problem
INNW	If Not Now, When
INPO	In No Particular Order
IOH	I Am Out Of Here / I'm Outta Here
IOMH	In Over My Head
ION	Index Of Names
IOUD	Inside, Outside, Upside Down
IOW	In Other Words
🚩 IPN	I Am Posting Naked
🚩 IRL	In Real Life

IRMC	I Rest My Case
ISAGN	I See A Great Need
ISH	Insert Sarcasm Here
ISLY	I Still Love You
ISO	In Search Of
ISS	I Said So / I'm So Sure
ISSYGTI	I'm So Sure You Get The Idea
ISTM	It Seems To Me
ISTR	I Seem To Remember
ISWYM	I See What You Mean
ISYALS	I'll Send You A Letter Soon
ITA	I Totally Agree
ITFA	In The Final Analysis
ITIGBS	I Think I'm Going To Be Sick
ITM	In The Money
⚑ ITS	Intense Text Sex
ITSFWI	If The Shoe Fits Wear It
ITYK	I Thought You Knew
IUM	If You Must
IUSS	If You Say So
IWALU	I Will Always Love You

IWBAPTAKYAIYSTA	I Will Buy A Plane Ticket And Kick Your Ass If You Say That Again
IWBNI	I Will Be Nice If...
IWIWU	I Wish I Was You
🚩 IWSN	I Want Sex Now
IYAOYAS	If You Ain't Ordinance You Ain't Shit
IYD	In Your Dreams
IYFEG	Insert Your Favorite Ethnic Group
IYKWIM	If You Know What I Mean
IYKWIM-AITYD	If You Know What I Mean And I Think You Do
IYO	In Your Opinion
IYQ	I Like You
IYQ2	I Like You Too
IYSS	If You Say So
IYSWIM	If You See What I Mean
🚩 J	Joint / Marijuana
J2LYK	Just To Let You Know
J4F	Just For Fun
J4G	Just For Grins
J4T	Just For Today

J5M	Just Five Minutes
JAD	Just Another Day
🚩 JAFO	Just Another F**king Onlooker
🚩 JAFS	Just Another F**king Salesman
JAM	Just A Minute
JAS	Just A Second
JC	Jesus Christ / Just Checking / Just Chilling/ Just Curious /
JDI	Just Do It
🚩 JEOMK	Just Ejaculated On My Keyboard
JFF	Just For Fun
🚩 JFGI	Just F**king Google It
🚩 JFH	Just F**k Her
JFI	Just For Information
JFT	Just For Today
JIC	Just In Case
JJ	Just Joking
JJA	Just Joking Around
JK	Just Kidding
JLY	Jesus Loves You
JM2C	Just My 2 Cents
JMO	Just My Opinion

🚩 JO	Jag Off / Jerking Off
JOOTT	Just One Of Those Things
🚩 JOS	Just Oral Sex
JP	Just Playing
JSU	Just Shut Up
JSYK	Just So You Know
🚩 JT	Just Teasing / Juvenile Trolling
JTLYK	Just To Let You Know
JTOL	Just Thinking Out Loud
JTOU	Just Thinking Of You
JUADLAM	Jumping Up And Down Like A Monkey
JW	Just Wondering
🚩 JWP	Juvenile With Papers
K	OK
K4Y	Kills For You
KB	Key Board or Kick Butt
KBD	Key Board
KEWL	"Cool"
KEYA	I Will Key You Later
KEYME	Key Me (When You Can)
KFY	Kiss For You

KHYF	Know How You Feel
KIA	Killed In Action
KIBO	Knowledge In, Bullshit Out
KIR	Keep It Real
KISS	Keep It Simple Stupid
KIT	Keep In Touch
KITTY	Vagina
KK	Kiss Kiss / Knock Knock
KMA	Kiss My Ass
KMBA	Kiss My Black Ass
KMFHA	Kiss My Fat Hairy Ass
KMP	Keep Me Posted
KMRIA	Kiss My Royal Irish Arse
KMSLA	Kiss My Shiny Little Ass
KMUF	Kiss Me You Fool
KMWA	Kiss My White Ass
KNIM	Know What I Mean
KOC	Kiss On the Cheek
KOK	Knock
KOL	Kiss On the Lips
KOTC	Kiss On The Cheek

🚩	KOTL	Kiss On The Lips
🚩	KPC	Keeping Parents Clueless
	KS	Kill Stealer
	KUTGW	Keep Up The Good Work
	KWIM	Know What I Mean
🚩	KWSTA	Kiss With Serious Tongue Action
	KYFC	Keep Your Fingers Crossed
	KYPO	Keep Your Pants On
	L	Laugh
	L33T	"LEET" or Elite
	L8R	Later
	L8RG8R	Later Gator
	LABATYD	Life's A Bitch And Then You Die
	LAQ	Lame Ass Quote
🚩	LB?WC	Like Bondage? Whips or Chains
🚩	LBIG	Laughing Because I'm Gay
	LBR	Little Boy's Room
🚩	LBUG	Laughing Because You're Gay
	LD	Long Distance / Later Dude
	LDIME	Look Deeply Into My Eyes
	LDR	Long Distance Relationship

	LDTTWA	Let's Do The Time Warp Again
	LEMENO	Let Me Know
	LERK	Leaving Easy Reach of Keyboard
🚩	LF	Let's F**k
	LFG	Looking For Group / Looking For Guard
	LFTI	Looking Forward To It
🚩	LGH	Let's Get High
	LGMAS	Lord Give Me A Sign
	LGR	Little Girl's Room
	LHM	Lord Help Me
	LHO	Laughing Head Off
🚩	LHOS	Let's Have Online Sex
	LIC	Like I Care
	LIFO	Last In, First Out
🚩	LIK	Liquor
🚩	LIQ	Liquor
	LIS	Laughing In Silence
	LJBF	Let's Just Be Friends
🚩	LKITR	Little Kid In The Room
🚩	LLOM	Like Leno On Meth
	LLTA	Lots and Lots of Thunderous Applause

LMAO	Laughing My Ass Off
LMBO	Laughing My Butt Off
🚩 LMFAO	Laughing My F**king Ass Off
LMHA	Laughing My Head Off
🚩 LMIRL	Let's Meet In Real Life
LMK	Let Me Know
LMNO	Leave My Name Out
LMSO	Laughing My Socks Off
LMTCB	Left Message To Call Back
LMTO	Laughing My Tits Off
LOL	Laughing Out Loud / Lots Of Love
LOLA	Laughing Out Loud Again
LOLH	Laughing Out Loud Hysterically
LOLO	LOts of LOve
🚩 LOMBARD	Lots Of Money But A Right Dick
LOML	Love of My Life
LONH	Lights On Nobody Home
LOOL	Laughing Outrageously Out Loud
LOPSOD	Long On Promises, Short On Delivery
LORE	Learn Once, Repeat Everywhere

	LOTR	Lord Of The Rings
	LOU	Laughing Over You
	LPOS	Lazy Piece Of Shit
	LQTM	Laughing Quietly To Myself
	LSHMBH	Laughing So Hard My Belly Hurts
⚑	LSV	Language, Sex, Violence
	LTHTT	Laughing Too Hard To Type
	LTIC	Laughing 'Til I Cry
	LTM	Laughing To Myself
	LTNS	Long Time No See
	LTNT	Long Time No Type
	LTR	Long Term Relationship
	LTS	Laughing To Self
⚑	LTTIC	Look The Teacher Is Coming
	LUL	Love You Lots
	LULU	Locally Undesirable Land Use
	LUMTP	Love You More Than Pie
	LUSM	Love You So Much
	LWOS	Laughing Without Smiling
⚑	LWR	Launch When Ready

	LY	Love You
	LY4FR	Love You Forever
	LYA	Love You All
	LYB	Love You Babe
	LYCYLBB	Love You, See You Later, Bye Bye
	LYKYAMY	Love You, Kiss You, Already Miss You
	LYL	Love You Lots
	LYLAB	Love You Like A Brother
	LYLAS	Love You Like A Sister
	LYLB	Love You, Later, Bye
	LYMI	Love You, Mean It
	LYSO	Love You So much
	LYWAMH	Love You With All My Heart
	M2NY	Me Too, Not Yet
🚩	M4C	Meet For Coffee
🚩	M4M	Men Looking for Men
🚩	M4S	Meet For Sex
🚩	M4W	Men Looking for Women
🚩	M8	Mate
	M	Male
🚩	MA	Mature Audiences

MAYA	Most Advanced Yet Accessible
MB	Message Board
MBN	Must Be Nice
🚩 MBRFN	Must Be Real F**king Nice
MC	Missed Connection
MEGO	My Eyes Glaze Over
meh	who cares, whatever
mehh	"sigh"
MFD	Multi-Function Device
MFI	Made For It
🚩 MFIC	Mother F**ker In Charge
MHBFY	My Heart Bleeds For You
MHOTY	My Hat's Off To You
🚩 MIA	Missing In Action
MIHYAP	May I Have Your Attention Please
MIL	Mother-In-Law
🚩 MILF	Mother I'd Like to F**k
🚩 MIRL	Meet In Real Life
MKOP	My Kind Of Place
MLAS	My Lips Are Sealed
MLM	Multi-Level Marketing

🚩 MM	Market Maker / Morning Missile (erection)	
MMHA2U	My Most Humble Apologies To You	
MO	Move On	
MOF	Matter Of Fact	
🚩 MOFO	Mother F**ker	
MOMPL	one Moment Please	
🚩 MOOS	Member Of the Opposite Sex	
MOP	MOment Please	
MorF	Male or Female	
🚩 MOS	Mom Over Shoulder	
🚩 MOSS	Member Of the Same Sex	
🚩 MOTAS	Member Of The Appropriate Sex	
MOTD	Message Of The Day	
🚩 MOTOS	Member Of The Opposite Sex	
🚩 MOTSS	Member Of the Same Sex	
🚩 MPFB	My Personal F**k Buddy	
MRA	Moving Right Along	
MS	Multi-Slacking	
🚩 MS	MySpace	
MSG	Message	

	MSMD	Monkey See Monkey Do
🚩	MSNUW	Mini Skirt No Under Wear
	MT	Multi-Tasking
	MTBF	Mean Time Before Failure
	MTF	More To Follow
	MTFBWY	May The Force Be With You
	MTLA	My True Love Always
	MTSBWY	May The Schwartz Be With You
	MUAH	Multiple Unsuccessful Attempts at Humor
🚩	MUBAR	Messed Up Beyond All Recognition
	MUSM	Miss You So Much
	MWAH	(the sound of a kiss)
	MWBRL	More Will Be Revealed Later
🚩	MYL	Mind Your Language
	MYOB	Mind Your Own Business
	N/A	Not Applicable
	N/M	Nothing Much
	N/T	No Text
	N1	Nice One
	N2M	Not To Mention / Not Too Much

N2MJCHBU	Not Too Much Just Chillin, How About You
NAB	Not A Blonde
NADT	Not A Damn Thing
NAK	Nursing At Keyboard
NALOPKT	Not A Lot Of People Know That
natch	Naturally
NAVY	Never Again Volunteer Yourself
NAYL	In A While
🚩 NAZ	Name, Address, Zip / Nasdaq
NB4T	Not Before Time
NBD	No Big Deal
NBFAB	Not Bad For A Beginner
NBIF	No Basis In Fact
NC	Nice Crib
NCG	New College Graduate
NDN	Indian / Native American
NE	Any
NE1	Anyone
NE14KFC	Anyone For KFC
NE1ER	Anyone Here
Ne2H	Need To Have

	NESEC	Any Second
	NEWS	North, East, West, South
🚩	NFBSK	Not For British School Kids
🚩	NFC	Not Favorably Considered / No F**king Chance
🚩	NFF	No F**king Fair
🚩	NFG	Not F**king Good
🚩	NFI	No F**king Idea
	NFM	Not For Me
🚩	NFS	Need For Speed / Not For Sale
🚩	NFW	No F**king Way / No Feasible Way
	NG	New Game
	NGB	Nearly Good Bridge
🚩	NH	Nice Hand / Nut Hugger (tight jeans)
	NHOH	Never Heard Of Him/Her
	NICE	Nonsense In Crappy Existence
🚩	NIFOC	Naked In Front Of Computer
	NIGYYSOB	Now I've Got You, You Son Of A Bitch
	NIH	Not Invented Here
	NIM	No Internal Message

NIMBY	Not In My Back Yard
NIMJD	Not In My Job Description
NIMQ	Not In My Queue
NIMY	Never In A Million Years
NINO	Nothing In, Nothing Out / No Input, No Output
NISM	Need I Say More
NITL	Not In This Lifetime
🚩 NIYWFD	Not In Your Wildest F**king Dreams
NLL	Nice Little Lady
NLT	No Later Than
NM	Never Mind / Nothing Much / Nice Move
NME	Enemy
NMH	Not Much Here
NMHJC	Not Much Here, Just Chilling
NMP	Not My Problem
NMTE	Now More Than Ever
NMU	Not Much, You
NN	Not Now
🚩 NNCIITFZ	Not Now Chief, I'm In The F**king Zone
NNWW	Nudge, Nudge, Wink, Wink

NO	Not Online
NOA	Not Online Anymore
NOFI	No Offense Intended
NO1	No One
noob	newbie
NOOB	New Gamer
NOS	New Old Stock
NOY	Not Online Yet
NOYB	None Of Your Business
⚑ NP	No Problem / Nosy Parents
⚑ NQA	No Questions Asked
NQOCD	Not Quite Our Class Dear
NQT	Newly Qualified Teacher
NR	Not Really / Nice Roll
NRG	Energy
NRN	No Reply Necessary
NS	Nice Set / Nice Score
NSA	No Strings Attached
NSFW	Not Safe For Work
NSISR	Not Sure If Spelled Right
NSS	No Shit Sherlock

 NSTLC	Need Some Tender Loving Care
NT	Nice Try
NTA	Not This Again
NTIM	Not That It Matters
NTIMM	Not That It Matters Much
NTK	Nice To Know
NTTAWWT	Not That There's Anything Wrong With That
NTW	Not To Worry
NTYMI	Now That You Mention It
NUB	Neophyte
NUCOSM	No Use Crying Over Spilt Milk
NUFF	Enough Said
NVM	Never Mind
NVNG	Nothing Ventured, Nothing Gained
NW	No Way
NWAL	Nerd Without A Life
NWO	No Way Out
NWR	Not Work Related
NYC	Not Your Concern
O	Opponent / Over
O2	Two Cents Worth

OAO	Over And Out
OATUS	On A Totally Unrelated Subject
OAUS	On An Unrelated Subject
OB	Obligatory / Oh Baby / Oh Brother
OBE	Overcome By Events
OBO	Or Best Offer
OBTW	Oh By The Way
OBX	Old Battle Axe
OC	Original Character
OCD	Obsessive Compulsive Disorder
ODTAA	One Damn Thing After Another
OIC	Oh I See
OICU812	Oh I See, You Ate One Too
OICURAQT	Oh I See You Are A Cutie
OK	All Correct / All Right
OL	Old Lady
⚑ OLL	Online Love
OLNTQT	Online Netiquette
OM	Old Man
OMDB	Over My Dead Body

OMG	Oh My God
OMGYG2-BK	Oh My God You Got To Be Kidding
OMIK	Open Mouth, Insert Keyboard
OML	Oh My Lord
OMW	On My Way
ONID	Oh No I Didn't
ONL	Online
ONNA	Oh No, Not Again
ONNTA	Oh No, Not This Again
ONUD	Oh No You Didn't
OO	Over and Out
OOAK	One Of A Kind
OOC	Out Of Character / Out Of Control
OOF	Out Of Facility
OOH	Out Of Here
OOI	Out Of Interest
OOO	Out Of Office
OOS	Out Of Stock
OOTB	Out Of The Box / Out Of The Blue
OOTC	Obligatory On Topic Comment

OOTD	One Of These Days
OOTO	Out Of The Office
OP	On Phone / Original Poster
ORLY	Oh Really
OSIF	Oh Shit I Forgot
OSINTOT	Oh Shit I Never Thought Of That
OST	On Second Thought
OT	Off Topic
OTASOIC	Owing To A Slight Oversight In Construction
OTB	Off To Bed / Off Track Bet
OTC	Over The Counter
OTF	On The Floor
OTFL	On The Floor Laughing
OTH	Off The Hook
OTL	Out To Lunch
OTOH	On The Other Hand
OTP	On The Phone
OTSP	On The Same Page
OTT	Over The Top
OTTOMH	Off The Top Of My Head
OTW	Off The Wall / Off To Work

	OUSU	Oh, You Shut Up
	OW	Or What?
	OWTTE	Or Words To That Effect
	P	Partner
🚩	P&C	Private & Confidential
	P2C2E	Process Too Complicated To Explain
	P2P	Parent To Parent / Peer To Peer / Pat To Play / Pay to Play
🚩	P911	Parent Alert
🚩	PA	Parent Alert
🚩	PAL	Parents Are Listening
	PANS	Pretty Awesome New Stuff
🚩	PAW	Parents Are Watching / Parents At Work
🚩	PAY	Peyote
	PB	Potty Break / Pretty Boy
🚩	PBB	Parent Behind Back
	PBEM	Play By Email
	PBJ	Peanut Butter and Jelly / Pretty Boy Jock
	PC	Player Character / Politically Correct
	PCM	Please Call Me
	PD	Public Domain

PDH	Pretty Damn Happy
PDOMA	Pulled Directly Out of My Ass
PDQ	Pretty Damn Quick
PDS	Please Don't Shout
PEBCAC	Problem Exists Between Chair And Computer
PEBCAK	Problem Exists Between Chair And Keyboard
PEEPS	People
PeFo	Personal Forum
PFA	Pulled From Ass / Please Find Attached
🚩 PFC	Pretty F**king Cold
🚩 PHAT	Pretty Hot And Tempting
PIAP	Pig In A Pantsuit
PIBKAC	Problem Is Between Keyboard And Chair
PICNIC	Problem In Chair, Not In Computer
PIF	Paid In Full
PIMP	Peeing In My Pants
PIMPL	Peeing In My Pants Laughing
🚩 PIN	Person In Need
🚩 PIR	Parent In Room
PITA	Pain In The Ass

PITME-MBOAM	Peace In The Middle East, My Brother Of Another Mother
PKMN	Pokemon
PLMK	Please Let Me Know
PLOKTA	Press Lots Of Keys To Abort
PLS	Please
PLU	People Like Us
PLZ	Please
🏴 PM	Private Message / Personal Message
PMBI	Pardon My Butting In
PMF	Pardon My French
PMFI	Pardon Me For Interrupting
PMFJI	Pardon Me For Jumping In
PMIGBOM	Put Mind In Gear Before Opening Mouth
PMJI	Pardon My Jumping In
PML	Pissing Myself Laughing
PMP	Peeing My Pants
PMSL	Pissed My Self Laughing
PNATMBC	Pay No Attention To the Man Behind the Curtin
PNCAH	Please, No Cursing Allowed Here

PND	Possibly Not Definitely / Personal Navigation Device	
🚩 PNP	Party and Play (Crystal Meth and Sex)	
PO	Piss Off	
POAHF	Put On A Happy Face	
POAK	Passed Out At Keyboard	
🚩 POMS	Parent Over My Shoulder	
PONA	Person Of No Account	
POOF	Good-bye, gone, disappeared; also seen as ::poof::	
🚩 POS	Parent Over Shoulder / Piece Of Shit	
POSC	Piece Of Shit Computer	
🚩 POSSLQ	Persons of the Opposite Sex Sharing Living Quarters	
POTD	Post Of The Day	
POTS	Plain Old Telephone System / Pat On The Shoulder	
POTUS	President Of The United States	
POV	Point Of View / Privately Owned Vehicle	
PP	People	
PPL	Pay-Per-Lead / People	
PRBLY	Probably	
🚩 PRON	Pornography	

🚩	PRT	Party
🚩	PRW	People Are Watching
🚩	PS	Post Script, Phone Sex
	PSA	Public Service Announcement
	PSO	Product Superior to Operator
🚩	PSOS	Parent Standing Over Shoulder
🚩	PT	Prick Teaser
	PTH	Prime Tanning Hours / Pimpin' The Hood
	PTL	Praise The Lord
	PTMM	Please Tell Me More
	PTP	Pardon The Pun
🚩	PTPOP	Pat The Pissed Off Primate
	PU	that stinks
	PUG	Pick Up Group
	PVP	Player Versus Player
	PWN	Own
	PWNT	Owned
	PWP	Plot, What Plot
	PXT	Please Explain That
	PZ	Peace
	PZA	Pizza
	Q	Queue

🚩	Q2C	Quick To Cum
	QFE	Question For Everyone / a fart
🚩	QFT	Quoted For Truth / Quit F**king Talking
	QIK	Quick
	QL	Quit Laughing
	QLS	Reply
	QOTD	Quote Of The Day
	QPQ	Quid Pro Quo (what's in it for me)
	QQ	Quick Question / crying eyes
	QS	Quit Scrolling
	QSL	Reply
	QSO	Conversation
	QT	Cutie
	QTPI	Cutie Pie
🚩	QuFo	Queer Forum
	QYB	Quit Your Bitching
	R&D	Research & Development
	R&R	Rest & Relaxation / Rants & Raves
	RAEBNC	Read And Enjoyed, But No Comment
🚩	RAT	Remotely Activated Trojan
	RB@Y	Right Back At Ya

	RBAY	Right Back At Ya
	RBTL	Read Between The Lines
	RC	Remote Control
🚩	RCH	Red C**t Hair (carpenter's smallest measurement)
	RCL	Rectal Cranial Inversion
	RE	Regarding / Reply
	REHI	hi again
	RFD	Request For Discussion
	RFL	Real Life Friend
🚩	RFR	Really F**king Rich
🚩	RFS	Real F**king Soon
	RGR	Roger
	RHIP	Rank Has Its Privileges
	RIYL	Recommended If You Like
	RKBA	Right to Keep and Bear Arms
🚩	RL	Real Life
🚩	RLCO	Real Life Conference
	RLY	Really
	RM	Remake
	RME	Rolling My Eyes
	RMLB	Read My Lips Baby

	RMMA	Reading My Mind Again
	RMMM	Read My Mail Man
	RN	Right Now
	RNN	Reply Not Necessary
	ROFL	Rolling On the Floor Laughing
🚩	RoFo	Romantic Forum
	ROTF-LMAO	Rolling On The Floor Laughing My Ass Off
	ROTM	Right On The Money
	RPG	Role Playing Games / Rocket Propelled Grenade
	RRR	haR haR haR (laughing out loud)
	RRRQ	Return Receipt Request
	RS	Runescape
	RSN	Real Soon Now / Raisin (old person)
	RSVP	Respond Please (respondez s'il vous plait)
🚩	RT	Real Time
	RT	ReTweet / ReTwitter
	RTBS	Reason To Be Single
	RTFAQ	Read The FAQs
🚩	RTFF	Read The F**king FAQs
🚩	RTFM	Read The F**king Manual

🚩	RTFQ	Read The F**king Question
	RTH	Release The Hounds
	RTK	Return To Keyboard
	RTM	Read The Manual
	RTSM	Read The Silly Manual
	RTTS	Right Thing To Say
🚩	RTWFQ	Read The Whole F**king Question
	RU	Are You
🚩	RU^18	Are You Over 18
🚩	RUFKM	Are You F**king Kidding Me
🚩	RUH	Are You Horny
	RUMCUMHMD	Are You on Medication Cuz You Must Have Missed a Dose
	RUMOF	Are You Male Or Female
	RUNL8	Running Late
	RUNTZ	Are You Nuts
	RUOK	Are You Okay
	RUS	Are You Serious
🚩	RUSOS	Are You SOS (in trouble)
	RUT	Are You There
	RUUP4IT	Are You Up For It
🚩	RX	Regards / Prescription

RYFM		Read Your Friendly Manual
🚩 RYO		Roll Your Own
RZN		Raisin (old person)
RYS		Read Your Screen
S		Smile
S^		What's Up
S2R		Send To Receive
S2U		Same To You
S4L		Spam For Life
🚩 SADAD		Suck A Dick And Die
SAHM		Stay At Home Mom
SAIA		Stupid Asses In Action
SAL		Such A Laugh
SAPFU		Surpassing All Previous Foul Ups
SBI		Sorry 'Bout It
SBT		Sorry 'Bout That
SBUG		Small Bald Unaudacious Goal
SC		Stay Cool
SCNR		Sorry, Could Not Resist
🚩 SDK		Scottie Doesn't Know / Software Developer's Kit/Selling Drugs to Kids
SEC		wait a Second

SED	Said Enough Darling
SEG	Shit Eating Grin
SEP	Someone Else's Problem
SETE	Smiling Ear To Ear
SEWAG	Scientifically Engineered Wild Ass Guess
SF	Surfer Friendly / Science Fiction
SFAIAA	So Far As I Am Aware
SFAIK	So Far As I Know
⚑ SFTTM	Stop F**king Talking To Me
SFX	Sound Effects / Stage Effects
SH	Shit Happens / Same Here
SHB	Should Have Been
SHID	Slapping Head In Disgust
SHMILY	See How Much I Love You
⚑ SHROOMZ	Hallucinogenic Mushrooms
SIC	Spelling Is Correct
SICL	Sitting In Chair Laughing
SICNR	Sorry I Could Not Resist
SIG2R	Sorry I Got To Run
SIHTT	Stupidity Is Hard To Take
SII	Seriously Impaired Imagination

SIL	Sister-In-Law
SIS	Snickering In Silence
SIT	Stay In Touch
SITCOM	Single Income, Two Children, Oppressive Mortgage
SITD	Still In The Dark
🚩 SIUP	Suck It Up Pussy
🚩 SIUYA	Shove It Up Your Ass
Sk8r	Skater
SL	Second Life
SLAP	Sounds Like A Plan
SLAW	Sounds Like A Winner
SLM	See Last Mail
SLOM	Sticking Leeches On Myself
SLRK	Smart Little Rich Kid
SLT	Something Like That
SM	Senior Moment
SMAIM	Send Me An Instant Message
🚩 SMB	Suck My Balls
SME	Subject Matter Expert
SMEM	Send Me Email
SMH	Shaking My Head
SMHID	Shaking My Head In Disbelief

	SMIM	Send Me An Instant Message
	SMOP	Small Matter Of Programming
🚩	SNAFU	Situation Normal, All F**ked Up
	SNAG	Sensitive New Age Guy
	SNERT	Snotty Nosed Egotistical Rude Teenager
🚩	SO	Significant Other (boyfriend, fiancé etc)
🚩	SOB	Son Of a Bitch
	SOBT	Stressed Out Big Time
🚩	SOG	Straight Or Gay
	SOGOP	Shit Or Get Off the Pot
	SOH	Sense Of Humor
	SOHF	Sense Of Humor Failure
	SOI	Self Owning Idiot
🚩	SOIAR	Sit On It And Rotate
	SOL	Shit Out of Luck
	SOMY	Sick Of Me Yet
🚩	SOOYA	Snake Out Of Your Ass
	SOP	Standard Operating Procedure
🚩	SorG	Straight Or Gay
	SOS	Same Old Shit
	SOT	Short On Time

SOTMG	Short On Time, Must Go
SOW	Speaking Of Which / Statement Of Work
🚩 SOWM	Some One With Me
SOZ	Sorry
SPK	Speak
SPST	Same Place Same Time
SPT	Spoke To
SPYNGTW	Stop Picking Your Nose, Get To Work
SRSLY	Seriously
SRY	Sorry
🚩 SS	Safe Sex / Sport Sex
SS	So Sorry
🚩 SSC	Super Sexy Cute
SSDD	Same Shit Different Day
SSDF	Same Shit Different Fly
SSEWBA	Someday Soon, Everything Will Be Acronyms
SSIA	Subject Says It All
SSIF	So Stupid It's Funny
SSINF	So Stupid It's Not Funny
ST&D	Stop Texting And Drive
STBY	Sucks To Be You

	STD	Seal The Deal
🚩	STFU	Shut The F**k Up
🚩	STFW	Search The F**king Web
🚩	STM	Spank The Monkey
🚩	STR8	Straight
	STS	So To Speak
	STW	Search The Web
	STYS	Speak To You Soon
	SU	Shut Up
	SUAC	Shit Up A Creek
	SUAKM	Shut Up And Kiss Me
🚩	SUFI	Super Finger / Shut Up F**king Imbecile
	SUFID	Screwing Up Face In Disgust
	SUITM	See You In The Morning
	SUP	What's Up
	SUYF	Shut Up You Fool
	SWAG	Scientific Wild Ass Guess
	SWAK	Sealed (Sent) With A Kiss
	SWALCAKWS	Sealed With A Lick Cuz A Kiss Won't Stick
	SWALK	Sealed With A Loving Kiss
	SWDYT	So What Do You Think

SWIM	See What I Mean
SWIS	See What I'm Saying
SWL	Screaming With Laughter
SWMBO	She Who Must Be Obeyed
SWU	So What's Up
SYL	See You Later
SYS	See You Soon
SYT	See You Tomorrow
T&C	Terms And Condition
T@YL	Talk At You Later
T+	Think Positive
TA	Thanks Again
TAF	That's All, Folks
TAFN	That's All For Now
TAH	Take A Hike
TAKS	That's A Knee Slapper
TAM	Tomorrow A.M.
TANJ	There Ain't No Justice
TANSTAAFL	There Ain't No Such Thing As A Free Lunch
TAP	Take A Pill
⚑ TARFU	Things Are Really F**ked Up

	TAS	Taking A Shower
	TAU	Thinking About You
🚩	TAW	Teachers Are Watching
🚩	TB	The Bird
	TBA	To Be Announced / To Be Advised
	TBC	To Be Continued
	TBD	To Be Determined
	TBE	Thick Between Ears
	TBH	To Be Honest
🚩	TBYB	Try Before You Buy
	TC	Take Care
	TCB	Taking Care of Business / Trouble Came Back
🚩	TD	Touch Down
	TDM	Too Darn Many
🚩	TD2M	Talk Dirty To Me
🚩	TDTM	Talk Dirty To Me
	TEOTWAWKI	The End Of The World As We Know It
	TFDS	That's For Damn Sure
	TFH	Thread From Hell
	TFLMS	Thanks For Letting Me Share

⚑	TFMIU	The F**king Manual Is Unreadable
	TFN	Thanks For Nothing / Til Further Notice
⚑	TFS	Thanks For Sharing / Three Finger Salute: CTRL + ALT + DEL or Female Masturbation
	TFTHAOT	Thanks For The Help Ahead Of Time
	TFTT	Thanks For The Thought
	TFX	Traffic
	TGAL	Think Globally, Act Locally
	TGGTG	That Girl/Guy has Got To Go
	TGIF	Thank God Its Friday
	TGIT	Thank God Its Thursday (4 day week)
	THKS	Thanks
	THMR	Thumber
	THNQ	Thank You
	THX	Thanks
	TIA	Thanks In Advance
	TIAD	Tomorrow Is Another Day
	TIAIL	Think I Am In Love
	TIC	Tongue In Cheek
	TIGAS	Think I Give A Shit
	TILII	Tell It Like It Is

TINWIS	That Is Not What I Said
TISC	This Is So Cool
TISL	This Is So Lame
TISNC	This Is So Not Cool
TISNF	That Is So Not Fair
TISNT	That Is So Not True
🚩 TK	To Come
TKU4UK	Thank You For Your Kindness
🚩 TL	Tool
TLC	Tender Loving Care
TLGO	The List Goes On
TLITBC	That's Life In The Big City
TLK 2 U-L8R	Talk To You Later
TM	Trust Me/ Tweet Me / Twitter Me
TMA	Too Many Acronyms
TMA	Tweet My Ass
TMB	Text Me Back
TMI	Too Much Information
TMOT	Trust Me On This
TMTH	Too Much To Handle
TMTOWTDI	There's More Than One Way To Do It

TMWFI	Take My Word For It
TNA	Temporarily Not Available
TNC	Tongue In Cheek
TNSTAAFL	There's No Such Thing As A Free Lunch
TNT	Til Next Time
TNTL	Trying Not To Laugh
TNX	Thanks
TOBAL	There Oughta Be A Law
TOBG	This Oughta Be Good
TOJ	Tears Of Joy
TOM	Tomorrow
TOPCA	Til Our Paths Cross Again
TOT	Tons Of Time
TOY	Thinking Of You
TP	Team Player / TelePort
TPC	The Phone Company
TPM	Tomorrow P.M.
TPS	That's Pretty Stupid
TPTB	The Powers That Be
TQM	Total Quality Management
TRAM	The Rest Are Mine
TRDMC	Tears Running Down My Cheeks

🚩 TS	Tough Shit / Tramp Stamp (tattoo on lower back)
TSIA	This Says It All
TSNF	That's So Not Fair
TSOB	Tough Son Of a Bitch
TSR	Totally Stuck in RAM / Totally Stupid Rules
TSRA	Two Shakes of a Rat's Ass
TSTB	The Sooner The Better
🚩 TT	Big Tease
🚩 TTA	Tap That Ass
TTBOMK	To The Best Of My Knowledge
TTFN	Ta Ta For Now
TTG	Time To Go
TTIOT	The Truth Is Out There
TTKSF	Trying To Keep a Straight Face
TTLY	Totally
🚩 TTMF	Ta Ta Mother F**ker
TTS	Text To Speech
TTT	That's The Ticket / To The Top / Thought That Too
TTTHTFAL	Talk To The Hand The Face Ain't Listening
TTTKA	Time To Totally Kick Ass
TTTT	To Tell The Truth / These Things Take Time

TTYAFN	Talk To You Awhile From Now
TTUL	Talk To You Later
TTWWADI	That's The Way We've Always Done It
TTYL	Talk To You Later
TTYS	Talk To You Soon
TTYT	Talk To You Tomorrow
TU	Thank You
TVM	Thanks Very Much
TWD	Texting While Driving
TWHAB	This Won't Hurt A Bit
TWIMC	To Whom It May Concern
TWIWI	That Was Interesting, Wasn't It
TXS	Thanks
TXT IM	Text Instant Message
TY	Thank You
TYCLO	Turn Your CAPS LOCK Off
TYSM	Thank You So Much
TYT	Take Your Time
TYVM	Thank You Very Much
U	You
U UP	Are You Up
U2	You Too

U8	You Ate
UBS	Unique Buying State
UCMU	You Crack Me Up
UCWAP	Up A Creek Without A Paddle
UDH82B-ME	You'd Hate To Be Me
🚩 UDI	Unidentified Drinking Injury
UFN	Until Future Notice
UG2BK	You've Got To Be Kidding
UKTR	You Know That's Right
UL	You Will / Upload
unPC	Politically Incorrect
UNTCO	You Need To Chill Out
UOK	Are You Okay
UPOD	Under Promise Over Deliver
UR	You Are
UR2K	You Are Too Kind
URAPITA	You Are A Pain In The Ass
🚩 URH	You Are Hot
URSAI	You Are Such An Idiot
URSKTM	You Are So Kind To Me
URTM	You Are The Man
URW	You Are Welcome

URWS	You Are Wise
URYY4M	You Are Too Wise For Me
US	You Suck
USC	Up Shits Creek
USP	Unique Selling Proposition
USUL	You Snooze You Lose
UTM	You Tell Me
🚩 UV	Unpleasant Visual
UW	You're Welcome
UWIWU	You Wish I Was You
VBG	Very Big Grin
VBS	Very Big Smile
VC	Venture Capital
VCDA	Vaya Con Dias, Amigo
VEG	Very Evil Grin
🚩 VFF	Very F**king Funny
VFM	Value For Money
VGC	Very Good Condition
VGH	Very Good Hand
VGN	Vegan / Vegetarian
VIP	Very Important Person
VM	Voice Mail

VN	Very Nice
VRBS	Virtual Reality Bull Shit
VRY	Very
VSC	Very Soft Chuckle
VSF	Very Sad Face
VWD	Very Well Done
VWP	Very Well Played
W	What
W/	With
W/END	Weekend
W/O	Without
W3	World-wide Web
W8	Wait
WAD	Without A Doubt
WAEF	When All Else Fails
🚩 WAFB	What A F**king Bitch
🚩 WAFM	What A F**king Mess
WAFS	Warm And Fuzzies
WAG	Wild Ass Guess
WAH	Working At Home
WAI	What An Idiot
WAJ	What A Jerk / What A Joke

🚩	WAK	What A Kiss
	WAM	Wait A Minute
	WAMBAM	Web Application Meets Brick And Mortar
	WAN2TLK	Want To Talk
🚩	WAREZ	Pirated Software
	WAS	Wait A Second
	WAWA	Where Are We At
	WAYD	What Are You Doing
🚩	WAYF	Where Are You From
🚩	WAYN	Where Are You Now
	WB	Welcome Back / Write Back
	WBS	Write Back Soon
	WC	Who Cares / Welcome
	WCA	Who Cares Anyway
	WD	Well Done
	WDALYIC	Who Died And Left You In Charge
	WDDD	Whoopee Doo Da Dey
	WDR	With Due Respect
	WDT	Who Does That
	WDYK	What Do You Know
	WDYMBT	What Do You Mean By That

WDYS	What Did You Say
WDYT	What Do You Think
WE	What Ever
WEG	Wicked Evil Grin
WETSU	We Eat This Shit Up
WF	Way Fun
WFM	Works For Me
WG	Wicked Grin
🚩 WGAFF	Who Gives A Flying F**k
WH5	Who, What, When, Where, Why
WIBAMU	Well, I'll Be A Monkey's Uncle
WIBNI	Wouldn't It Be Nice
WIIFM	What's In It For Me
WILCO	Will Comply
WIM	Woe Is Me
WIP	Work In Progress
WISP	Winning Is So Pleasurable
WIT	Wordsmith In Training
🚩 WITFITS	What In The F**k Is This Shit
WITP	What Is The Point
WITW	What In The World
WIU	Wrap It Up

WK	Week / Work
WKD	Weekend
WKEWL	Way Cool
WMHGB	Where Many Have Gone Before
WMMOWS	Wash My Mouth Out With Soap
WMPL	Wet My Pants Laughing
WNOHGB	Where No One Has Gone Before
WOA	Work Of Art
WOG	Wise Old Guy
WOMBAT	Waste Of Money, Brains And Time
WOOF	Well Off Older Folks
🚩 WOP	Without Papers
WOTAM	Waste Of Time And Money
WOTD	Word Of The Day
WP	Well Played
WRK	Work
WRT	With Regard To
WRUD	What Are You Doing
🚩 WSM	Women Seeking Men
🚩 WSW	Women Seeking Women
WT	Without Thinking

	WTB	Want To Buy
🚩	WTF	What The F**k / Want To F**k
🚩	WTFGDA	Way To F**king Go Dumb Ass
🚩	WTFH	What The F**king Hell
	WTG	Way To Go
🚩	WTGP	Want To Go Private? (Private Chat)
	WTH	What The Heck / What The Hell
	WTM	Who's The Man
	WTMI	Way Too Much Information
	WTN	What Then Now / Who Then Now
	WTS	Want To Sell
	WTSDS	Where The Sun Don't Shine
	WTSHTF	When The Shit Hits The Fan
	WTTM	Without Thinking Too Much
	WU	What's Up
	WUCIWUG	What You See Is What You Get
	WUF	Where You From
	WUWH	Wish You Were Here
🚩	WUWHIMA	Wish You Were Here In My Arms
🚩	WW	Woo Wop (Steal cocaine)
	WWGT	We Won't Go There

WWJD	What Would Jesus Do
WWNC	Will Wonders Never Cease
WWY	Where Were You
WWYC	Write When You Can
WX	Weather
🚩 WYCM	Will You Call Me
WYD	What You Doing
🚩 WYFM	Would You F**k Me
WYGAM	When You Get A Minute
🚩 WYGI-WYPF	What You Get Is What You Pay For
WYHAM	When You Have A Minute
WYLEI	When You Least Expect It
WYM	What do You Mean
WYP	What's Your Problem
🚩 WYRN	What's Your Real Name
WYS	Whatever You Say
WYSIWYG	What You See Is What You Get
WYSLPG	What You See Looks Pretty Good
WYT	Whatever You Think
WYWH	Wish You Were Here
WYWO	While You Were Out

X	Kiss
XI10	Exciting
XLNT	Excellent
XME	Excuse Me
XME?	Excuse Me?
XOXO	Kisses and Hugs
XQZT	Exquisite
🚩 XTC	Ecstasy
XUSM	Excuse Me
🚩 XYZ	Examine Your Zipper
Y	Why
Y2K	You're Too Kind
YA	Yet Another
YACC	Yet Another Calendar Company
YAFIYGI	You Asked For It You Got It
YAOTM	Yet Another Off Topic Message
YARLY	Yeah, Really
YAUN	Yet Another Unix Nerd
🚩 YBF	You've Been F**ked
YBIC	Your Brother In Christ
YBS	You'll Be Sorry

YBY	Yeah Baby Yeah
YBYSA	You Bet Your Sweet Ass
YCLIU	You Can Look It Up
YCMU	You Crack Me Up
YCT	Your Comment To
YDHAHOYA	You Don't Have A Hair On Your Ass
YDKM	You Don't Know Me
⚑ YEPPIES	Young Experimenting Perfection Seekers
YF	Wife
YG	Young Gentleman
YGBK	You Gotta Be Kidding
YGBSM	You Gotta Be Shitting Me
YGG	You Go Girl
YGLT	You're Gonna Love This
YGTBK	You've Got To Be Kidding
⚑ YGWYPF	You Get What You Pay For
YHM	You Have Mail
YIC	Yours In Christ
YIU	Yes, I Understand
⚑ YIWGP	Yes, I Will Go Private
YKW	You Know What

YKWIM	You Know What I Mean
YKWYCD	You Know What You Can Do
YL	Young Lady
YM	Your Mother
YMAK	You May Already Know
YMMV	Your Mileage May Vary
YNK	You Never Know
YOOS	You're Out Of Sugar
YOYO	You're On Your Own
YR	Yeah Right / You're Right
YROYOCC	You're Running On Your Own Cuckoo Clock
YS	You Stinker
YSAN	You're Such A Nerd
YSIC	Why Should I Care / Your Sister In Christ
YSK	You Should Know
YSYD	Yeah, Sure You Do
YT	You There
YTB	You're The Best
YTG	You're The Greatest
YTRNW	Yeah That's Right, Now What
YTTT	You Telling The Truth

YUPPIES	Young Urban Professionals	
YW	You're Welcome	
YWIA	You're Welcome In Advance	
YY4U	Too Wise For You	
YYSSW	Yeah Yeah Sure Sure Whatever	
Z	Zero	
ZA	Pizza	
🚩 zerg	to gang up on someone	
🚩 ZOT	Zero Tolerance	
ZUP	What's Up	
ZZZ	Sleeping, Bored. Tired	

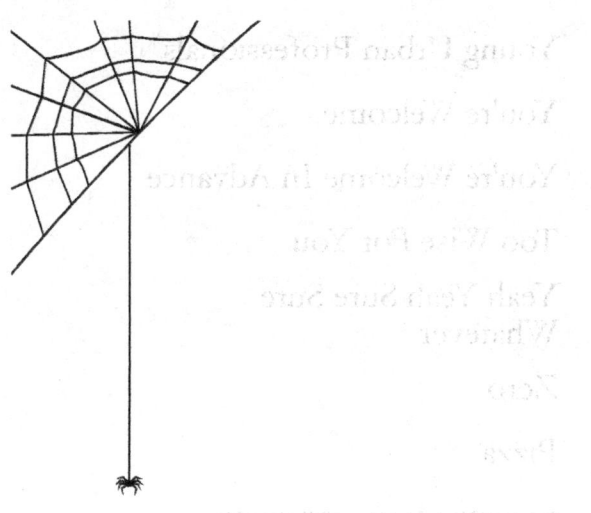

Beware!

Webs Have Spiders!

One of the greatest things about the World-wide Web is that it's world-wide. It's amazing what you can learn and who you can meet online. Scientific, medical, entertainment, art, sports...the world is literally a cornucopia of information, at your fingertips, twenty-four hours a day; most of it up to date information.

Paradoxically, what you can learn and who you can meet can be two of the greatest dangers on the internet. The solution is to become street smart on the information highway. While the advantages outweigh the risks, it is only prudent to safeguard yourself and your family against all dangers.

The joys of the internet far out-distance and over shadow the negatives. This is a great new world of adventure that we couldn't even begin to imagine a few short decades ago. But, like the language it has produced, the internet is both simple and complex... a wondrous paradox.

Embrace it. Most of all understand it for what it can do to enrich your life. You're not just in your own town anymore; you're instantly in New York, Chicago, Tokyo, Paris, Moscow, Algiers, Sydney, Hong Kong...and on some websites, you can instantly tour the galaxy. The opportunities are absolutely endless. Enjoy, but be safe.

World-wide Web Pitfalls

Chat Room Safety

- First of all, the vast majority of people you will meet online are not going to be a friend of a friend or a friend of a shoestring relative. Remember that every one you meet is NOT a friend of your family.

- Unsupervised children are most at risk. A child should never be allowed in a chatroom. A red flag should go up instantly if an online buddy wants to meet children anywhere in person. If you or your children are uncomfortable by an internet stranger, sever the relationship NOW! There are six billion people in the world. You will not be lonely if you forego this one contact.

- Never give out personal information. It may put you in danger. Financial data, your real name, Social Security number, address, phone numbers, school, names of friends, clubs, vulnerabilities such as age, family problems, health problems, photos of yourself, your family or your friends are ALL OFF LIMITS.

- Use an untraceable nick name. Never agree to meet in person, and if you do, only meet in a very public place, never go alone and make sure the other party sees that you're not alone.

- Another extremely important point to remember is that

anything you post on the internet has the possibility of being seen by millions of people. Be sure that what you do online is something that you will be proud of, or you would not be ashamed to do out in public. Pictures, videos, and messages can haunt you far into the future. We've heard of people who were not hired by big companies because of what they had posted on the internet years earlier.

Auction Safety

- Always stay within the bounds of the auction company. Selling or purchasing an item outside of the auction can lead to problems.

- Never agree to ship an item until you have proof that you've received cleared funds beforehand. Not just deposited, but cleared. Only use reputable and secure online payment systems. These are online companies that will, for a fee, receive funds online and transfer the funds into your account for you, or into a secure, reputable escrow account. They can also send payments online from your account, at your request, to another party's account on your behalf. You can also accept checks and money orders, but don't ship anything out until your bank assures you that the funds have been successfully transferred into your account.

- Never accept a buyer's word that they've deposited money into an escrow account where you can't see it or have it securely verified. Never accept "I have a letter of credit". Don't fall for legal phraseology such as "stand-by letter of credit" or "certified escrow".

- Always mark your item in an inconspicuous way. Keep a photograph for your files, so that you can prove if an item which has been returned to you as defective is actually the item you sent to them and not their own item that they're looking for you to replace for free. You can buy markers with ultraviolet ink, (some with built-in ultraviolet lights) that, when you mark with them, the ink is invisible and will only appear under ultraviolet light. That way no one can see where you marked the item but you.

- Don't listen to sob stories or to financial arrangements that sound too good to be true. Again, the internet is a wonderful place, but the opportunities for people to try to scam you are innumerable. It's much easier and more comfortable for them to scam you when you're not face-to-face. Always trust your feelings.

Identity Breaches

- There are common scams, with many creative variations, where you receive an email supposedly from a company that you trust, it may look official with logos, letterheads, ads and more. But these very official emails will ask you to verify personal information. Red flags should pop up in your head at once!

- Never email any personal information to anyone even if you have asked that particular company to contact you. NEVER give personal information through unsecured email. Delete the email or report it as spam. Call the company and ask if they've sent you an email, then ask for their secured site.

- NEVER give out your password! The word 'password' itself denotes safety and security — keep it that way. NEVER give out your password!

- There are so many scams and so many scammers online that it's best to distrust everything that shows up in your inbox that you personally did not ask for... just click on the "Delete" button!

Misinformation and Due Diligence

- Every one has an opinion, and they're not all correct. Verify data. Go to several different sites on the same topic and compare information before making decisions.

- Misinformation can be well-meaning or deliberate. It doesn't matter. Make up your own mind after you do your own research on several sites. Always double and triple check.

Vulnerability of Naïve Trust

- It's not just children who are naïve; we are all naïve when listening to something we want to hear. Stand back, take a minute, and take another look. There are lots of people out there who know what makes people like you and I tick, and they are eager to take advantage of us.

- Beware of statements requiring immediate action on your part or the deal/offer will be retracted.

- Remember that paranoia can be good when relating to some experiences online.

- When our children are on the internet, they become greater targets for unscrupulous and evil people. Talk to your children. Educate them on what you've learned. Show them that you too have been vulnerable at times. Never tolerate abusive language, bullying, or claims that are too good to be true. Educate your children on all these points as well; which brings us to...

Criminals and Charlatans

- Criminals cannot abuse you on the internet without your permission! That thought should empower you. Name, rank and serial number (unlike in the military) are never appropriate information. Don't get tricked into "deals" you feel may be wrong.

- Respect other's privacy. Copyright infringements are illegal acts that lead to trouble. Artists, authors, writers, musicians, etc., deserve to get paid for their work. More importantly, most will prosecute. Can you blame them?

Sexual Predators

- This is a problem more prevalent than you may think. We need to be aware of the dangers, or risk becoming another statistic. Proceed with caution!

- Any lonely person going on the internet for companionship is a target. Go ahead and chat with people, make friends, but if you want to go further than that, make very, very, very sure that this person is just who he/she says that he/she is. If you do decide to meet, don't go alone, never go alone the first time, and be sure to go somewhere very public.

- One of our relatives who had corresponded online with a man for several months had a bad experience when it came to MIRL (Meet In Real Life). They shared info, photos, likes, dislikes and more. When they finally did meet, at a very popular and busy restaurant, she was appalled with who showed up to the dinner date. This gentleman was so unlike how he had portrayed himself that she felt totally humiliated. She wasn't looking for a "hunk", but he was so different from the photos and his descriptions of himself, she was embarrassed that she had been duped. This online relationship had gone on for several months, and after all that time she could not believe she'd been deceived. She is far from being the only person ever fooled in this way. She did say later on that she was naïve, but giggled that it was better being deceived, than dismembered. She has since changed her online ways. Always be wary!

Unbelievable Product Claims

- The perfect old axiom to remember, "If it sounds too good to be true, it usually is too good to be true". When you buy online, it's the same as in a store--*caveat emptor*--buyer beware! Just as in stores made of brick and mortar, you get what you pay for, is the general rule. Have realistic expectations. Ask questions before buying.

- Online retailers need to make an honest profit in order to stay in business, but don't be taken advantage of by unscrupulous buyers or sellers.

Mobility of Online Contacts

- Reality check. Whether across the street or across the globe, the online environment is constantly changing and reinventing itself. Be Alert!

- If you bought a diamond from an online retailer, we would advise and hope that you would check the company or person out before purchasing. The screen name or email address you just sent money to could disappear tomorrow along with your hard earned cash.

- The same could be said for the "true love" you met online.

- "Mail Us Your Gold" is all the rage. Check out any company who offers you the "best deal". Remember what your mother told you, and deal with people you can trust. You may be better off dealing with your locally known jeweler, or a reputable gold party representative.

- Keep your money and your heart to yourself unless time and circumstances have warranted your faith. Perform your own due diligence, as legal experts advise.

Other Countries' Laws

- If you're going to live in the world, which you certainly do in an online environment, you have to know the world. It's not just the monetary rate that fluctuates.

- Take nothing for granted. Just because your American

laws give you protection here, nothing outside of the U.S. is guaranteed. When sending an item to another country, make sure the item is legal to be exported and/or imported.

- Ask Yourself... Can I be assured of getting my money or my product? How long will it take? Is the transaction clearly understood by both parties? This is where looking into online escrow accounts such as PayPal can ease your fears. They are there to make your transaction safer and for that they charge a reasonable fee.

- Conversely, when buying, ask, is this product legal in my country? An example being a national treasure that legally cannot leave their country, or a product that is legal there but not here.

- Are we, as a country, in a good relationship with this country: Do I have reasonable expectations of fair play being enforceable?

In all the above instances... remember what Mother said... trust your feelings, never give out information, and do your due diligence! Make all your experiences safe and fun!

Protecting Your Children Online

- It is imperative that we are cognizant of our children's online habits. Talk with your children so they understand that you want their online experiences to be fun and informative, but above all, you want them to be safe. Explain your rules to your children as you go so they can understand and appreciate the reasoning behind them.

- Keep the computer centrally located in plain view where online activity can be monitored, and not secluded in their bedrooms. Get in the habit of hitting the back button on the computer so you can see the last page your child viewed, and so your child understands that you will be checking on their activity. Watch for other pages that may be minimized to the taskbar (the bar at the very bottom of the screen). You can also see what sites have recently been opened by the drop down menu on the address bar.

- Limit your child's online time and access. Free reign can be inviting problems.

- Instruct your child to show you any emails or instant messages that make them feel even the tiniest bit uncomfortable, and then immediately report any suspicious activity, instant messages or email to authorities.

- Keep tabs on your child's online activities and buddy lists. Make your child's buddy list with your child and block all other access. Talk with them about their experiences with their online activities and friends.

- Never allow your child to enter a chatroom, especially an un-monitored chatroom. Even with monitoring, predators are still able to disguise who they are and freely interact with children unimpeded. Most parental controls and filters offer an option to block access to chatrooms.

- Never allow your child to have an online profile. This is the fastest way for a child predator to zero in on your child.

- An exception to this might be the children's website www.whyville.com. This website is designed to be set up by parents, for their children. They can have friends, earn virtual money, make music, and much more, but it is totally controlled by the parents.

- Internet providers have built-in parental controls and filters. There are many software programs available that can help to keep your child's online experience a safer one. The safest access is with a closed secure system which allows your children's access only to websites you have pre-selected.

- There are many online sites devoted to internet safety of all kinds for children and adults. We encourage everyone to check out these websites: www.fbi.gov; www.ftc.gov; www.kidshealth.org; www.mcgruff.org; www.missingkids.com;

www.netsmartz.org; www.protectkids.com; www.safekids.com; and many more, just keep searching. Let your children help you search and then read the information out loud to you.

- Many of these websites and other websites have printable parent/child contracts for agreeing how you and your child will treat their online time. You can also make a list of what is and what is not acceptable online behavior. Keep your list taped to or nearby the computer monitor as a constant reminder.

- Our research has shown that 20% to 25% of all children online will be approached by a child predator either in a chatroom or by instant message or email. There are millions of children online every day. If your child spends a lot of time online, the possibility of your child being contacted by a predator is astounding.

- We've found that it's to everyone's benefit to have your children not only watch out for internet predators for themselves, but to be aware of the warning signs concerning their friends' online relationships as well. Your children should feel empowered to help, should a friend or sibling get caught up in something that could be dangerous; feeling trapped with no one to turn to. Your child should report to you if he/she recognizes any of the warning signs on their friend's or sibling's computer, or with their activity, so that you can alert the child's parents. The proper authorities should be notified immediately, in case they need to monitor the situation or take action. Explain to your child that he/she isn't snitching. They could actually be saving a friend from a dangerous situation, being kidnapped, molested, or worse - killed.

"Sexting"

A phenomenon that seems to be gaining popularity among very young teens to young adults is Sexting. This term was previously used by adults to refer to the act of exchanging instant messages of an explicit sexual nature, mostly used to build excitement at the possibility of a sexual encounter in the future. The term Sexting is now being used by teens to describe the act of sending explicit messages, and/or photos and videos of themselves semi-nude or nude to others by way of their cell phones.

The numbers that survey takers have compiled from teens across the country are hard to believe. In one survey by The National Campaign to Prevent Teen and Unplanned Pregnancy, out of 1,280 teens and young adults, 20% admitted they had posted explicit photos or videos on the internet or sent them by cell phone. The number is slightly higher for teenage girls than teenage boys. PARENTS BEWARE! One in five students surveyed participates in Sexting!

The problem has gotten to the point where child pornography laws have come into play. No one wants to send an immature teenager to jail as a sex offender for what amounts to impaired morals, poor taste, and a lack of judgment. Most of the cases that have been in the news lately are just that.

Vermont's Legislature is considering a bill that would allow teenagers to send an image of himself/herself to a girlfriend/boyfriend without fear of child pornography charges if they are both at least 13 and under the age of 18, and the act is consensual. Officials feel that lesser charges on the books will curtail the practice, when applied, such as lewd and lascivious conduct. This will not absolve non-consensual sharing of images, nor will it protect those over 17 who send images to anyone under 18.

As mentioned in another chapter, young people have no concept of what these acts can mean to them later in life. If an unscrupulous person gets hold of these photos and posts them on the web, realistically they can stay there forever, and come back to haunt the person later in life.

It is possible for a 17-year-old caught with such photos, in a State that offers no leeway, to be convicted of possessing child pornography. Adolescents don't stop to think what a conviction can do to their future…the result can be devastating. With the ease of availability of information on the internet, corporate human resource departments, organizations, political entities, news media, credit companies, prestigious private schools, future spouses and more, much more, can and will look into every aspect of a person's history.

Personal Thoughts…

A lifetime of registering as a sex offender, coupled with incarceration is unconscionable for this offense, yet we believe it cannot be treated like jay-walking. When you are old enough to think sexually you are old enough to respect your sexuality and the ramifications thereof; i.e.: loss of reputation, unplanned pregnancy, sexually transmitted diseases, loss of spiritual morays and self-worth.

Complacent parenting and the unwillingness of the generations of late to accept personal responsibility, has everything to do with our degenerating morals and lack of values. We find it a sad sign of the times that during an interview, one mother when referring to her 13-year-old daughter's sexting, attempted to diminish any immorality by rationalizing that her daughter had "only" sent it to her boyfriend. (paraphrased)

Cyberbullying
A dangerous issue facing our children.

Until now, only tough guys could be bullies. It doesn't take a strong fist, only your thumbs, to deliver a knock out. Today's thumbers, no matter how slight of build, can be more intimidating than the ripped bully of old. The challenges that once were made on the playground are now delivered in secrecy and even anonymity into the sanctuary of your home.

These messages can take the form of threats, innuendos, exposed secrets, rumors, ridicule, distorted personal information, exposed embarrassing situations, or untrue information placed on websites such as MySpace and Facebook. Hacking into your account and sending other people hurtful messages using your name can also be done maliciously.

Young minds can be so tormented by these thumbers that if given their druthers, they'd prefer a playground pummeling to an emotional punch. Unfortunately, physical wounds heal, mental wounds may scar.

In effect, these actions can destroy your child's self esteem, cause anxiety and/or depression, and result in poor school performance and diminished social interaction.

Monitor your children's activities and their friends. Remind your children that The Golden Rule applies here…never send anything that you would be uncomfortable receiving.

Safe Thumbing

Some "thumbers" can text with their eyes closed. Some can accurately text behind their backs, which is cool, but TWD (Texting While Driving) can be deadly. Don't let a careless moment ruin your life or the lives of others, and possibly subject yourself to imprisonment. Just as in drunk driving, it's been proven that reaction times are impaired.

Whenever driving, don't take your brain off the wheel! Police are reporting that accidents caused by TWD are on the rise. Although the numbers for these accidents are getting higher, the figures remain somewhat skewed, because most texting is done below window level and is usually undetectable. Many automobile deaths have been attributed to TWD. One of the worst we are aware of is the deaths of five teens in which phone records suggest the driver may have been texting at the time of the accident.

The very worst is the horrific Los Angeles train collision between a Metrolink commuter train and a Union Pacific engine on 9/12/08 that killed 25 people, including the engineer, and injured at least 135 others. The National Transportation Safety Board is investigating the cause of the accident. They know that the engineer of the commuter train ran a red signal just before the collision. Two teenagers have allegedly reported that they received text messages from that engineer just moments before the collision.

Aside from TWD, other safety issues include texting while

walking, while using stairways, while crossing the street, around trains, etc. Hospital reports indicate that it's not only the texter who can be injured by this careless distraction; others in the proximity of an inattentive texter can get hurt by colliding with, or trying to evade, the texter.

In many areas, TWD is already against the law... and the trend is growing. Some statistics show that TWD can diminish reaction time by 30% or more. This assertion translates to a greater chance that a thumber will be caught TWD, and with possibly disastrous results. We have to ask ourselves...could any message be that important?

STAY ALIVE—DON'T TEXT AND DRIVE!

Your Brain On Twitter

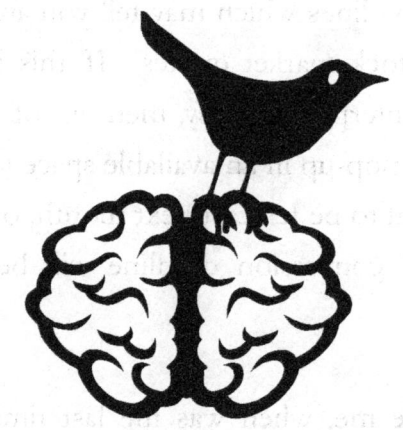

"Warning! Warning! Situation Dangerous, Will Robinson!"

"Red Alert! Red Alert!" "Input Overload!" "Does Not Compute!"

Like the robot on the classic 1960s TV show "Lost In Space", today's multi-tasking, multi-knowledge, and event absorbing tendencies of our modern society is in overload status.

When you view the TV screen on a news program today it looks like this: You'll find the newscaster in center front, above left you may find the word LIVE, above right may be a program logo. The bottom left may have a digital clock, whereas the bottom right may show the channel. Now underneath this may be one to three crawl lines which may tell you anything from breaking news to stock market quotes. If this isn't enough to keep a team of interpreters busy, then out of nowhere an animated teaser will pop-up in an available space to tell you of the upcoming special to be telecast next month, or a reminder that the digital TV conversion deadline will be postponed again.

If you don't believe me, when was the last time you saw - through the digital overload maze - a golf ball actually drop into the cup during a Tiger Woods highlight?

Let's take a look at your computer screen in "You Gots":

You got the Web Page Banner
"   "   "   Internet Bar (no drinks served)
"   "   "   Address Bar
"   "   "   Search Bar
"   "   "   Variety of Menus (no appetizers)
"   "   "   Information Banner
"   "   "   Moving Ad Banners
"   "   "   Array of Tabs
"   "   "   Gaggle of Links to Click On (Oh pick me! Pick me!)

….and the list goes on. Thank God they usually have a 'Help' button somewhere on the page.

Now, let us assess the cell phone…It's like how did Contadina put those 8 great tomatoes into that itty-bitty can? The small screens have limited viewing surface, yet the abuse goes on: Menu, Phone Book, Contacts, Messages, Net, Settings, Camera, Pictures, Music Player, and you may even find "Where's Waldo?"

Recent theories now espouse rapid digital media absorption may be hazardous to your morality. Huh? Yeah, that's what we thought. Well, if you are a heavy user of digital media devices, you just may be desensitizing yourself.

It appears that information is presented so swiftly that you don't have the time to react normally and to feel and internalize tragedies and adverse circumstances. Your brain tends to become numb to the fact that the President's new Portuguese Water puppy was squished beneath Helicopter One. (Just a tragic example, PETA.)

This theory is of the opinion that one's normal human response can become impaired and may lead to anxiety disorders. It is being said that actual brain scans have shown imaging alterations from the effects of a rapid stream of visual and audio intake.

The best way not to suffer these effects is to separate the components and set aside time for each of your electronic intakes. Don't Twitter, email, MySpace, FaceBook, text, or receive news intake, all day long, or multi-absorb the mix. If you work with each activity in its own timeframe, you will be able to enjoy each more and suffer the ill effects less. Maybe one of the big drug companies can develop a patch for electronic media addiction, instead of later treating them with anti-anxiety pills. Just watch someone who checks for email or text messages every 90 seconds. Can you spell A-N-X-I-E-T-Y?

Be Forgiving

The message you send intending the best of times, can be received and misinterpreted causing the worst of times. Intentions can be misconstrued. Words converted by thumbing SMS text messages are sent with the best of intentions. That same message, received from cyberspace, can take on an inaccurate interpretation once articulated.

Language has a cadence, an inflection that indicates as much as the words themselves. Read your written communication aloud to yourself to avoid hurt feelings or misunderstandings.

For example, simply texting the comment "Yeah, right." You could send it meaning "Yeah, you make a good point and you are so right. Thanks for your input." But it could easily be misread as "Yeah right, like that's going to happen."

Here are a couple examples we learned second hand: One of our friends, new to thumbing, sent a text message to his girlfriend that was summarily misinterpreted, causing her hurt feelings. Our friend had to personally verbalize his meaning in order to correctly relay what he actually intended to say. We also know of a married couple whose text messages were also misunderstood and caused the couple to stop speaking for a week. Yes, one week, until the true meanings were finally correctly conveyed.

We feel compelled to mention the famous celebrity faux pas... Jennifer Aniston was unceremoniously dumped by former boyfriend John Mayer through a short and abrupt text message.

And in our town, local gossip has it, that a neighbor sent text messages to his wife and his daughter communicating to them, that because his interests had changed, his life was taking a new direction with a new person and he wouldn't be coming back home. (Paraphrased)

It's truly amazing that individuals can be so unkind to those they previously cared about; but they can, as long as they have their cell phones to hide behind. Such callousness is unimaginable to most of us. Texting has many great applications, but blantant, and hurtful cruelty should not be among them.

Medical Alert

A serious issue being addressed lately by the media is the possible rise of brain tumors and cancers associated with cell phone usage. New studies are showing a strong probability that cell phones are hazardous to your health because of the radiation emanating from them, similar to the radiation emitted by microwave ovens. We can understand this, knowing how hot these phones can become from a lengthy phone conversation. It's been noted that text messaging and utilizing the speakerphone option available on most cell phones are safer ways of communicating because the cell phone is not held to your head, thus limiting exposure to radiation. The jury is still out on headsets, as some schools of thought contend that they may actually attract radiation from other sources nearby.

Studies have also demonstrated that the younger the person, the more readily the radiation is absorbed. The developing brain is more susceptible because the young skull is thinner and there is more water in the younger brain to absorb radiation. This type of radiation is not the same as used in x-rays, and long term exposure has not been sufficiently studied to determine the risks.

The cell phone has become our mobile office, our companion, our security blanket…our link to the world. We are not going to give them up; "not from our cold dead hands!" As with the internet, the benefits far outweigh the risks… risks that we need to be aware of, and then take the proper steps to minimize any possible harmful effects.

Metaphors For:
Drunk On Alcohol

3 Sheets	Numsy-Faced
Annihilated	On the Sauce
Bagged	Pickled
Basted	Plastered
Blasted	Plowed
Blitzed	Polluted
Blotto	Primed
Bombed	Ripped
Boozed Up	Sauced
Calling Europe	Shitfaced
Crocked	Skunked
Drunk	Sloshed
Fried	Smashed
Gassed	Snockered
Gone	Soused
Half in the Bag	Stiff
Hammered	Stinko
In the Bag	Tanked
Inebriated	Tipsy
Intoxicated	Toasted
Jacked	Totalled
Juiced	Trashed
Lit	Wasted
Loaded	

Metaphors For:
High On Drugs

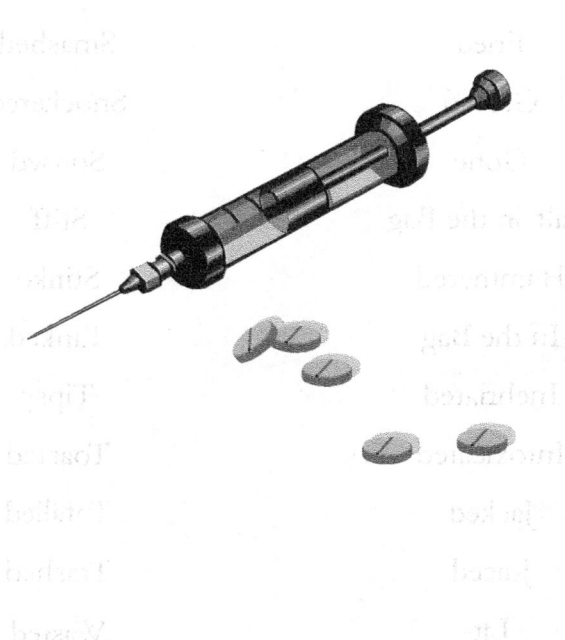

Acid Head	Doobagged
Air Headed	Druggie
All Lit Up	E-Bombed
Amped	E-Puddled
Ampin	E-Tard
Bagged	Fired Up
Baked	Fishin' Out
Beamered	Flashback
Belted	Flatlining
Blasted	Flipping Out
Blazed	Floating
Bombed Out	Flying
Burned Out	Freaked Out
Buzzed	Fried
CB	Ganoobies
Charred the Dragon	Gassed
Chiefed	G-Ber Dazed
Chippered	Geeked
Circled	Geeking
Coasting	Get Off
Coocoo on Cocoa Puffs	Glued
Crashing	Gone
Crunked	Got the Munchies
Did Shit	Grooving

HammerHeading
Has Yellow Fever
Heading
Heavy Burner
High
Hippie Flipped
Holding
Hooked
Hopped Up
Huffered
Ice Creamer
In the Gallery
In the O-Zone
Jacked
Jagged
Joy Popping
Junked
Junkie
K-Holed
Kickbacked
K-Whore
Lit Up
Loaded
Main Lined

Melting down
Mezzed Up
Mind Blown
Monkied
Mowed the Grass
Nex Flipping
Nexus Flipping
OD-ing
On
On a Trip
On Pepsi One
On Rocket Fuel
On the Needle
On the Nod
Out of Body Experience
Out of It
Parachuting
Pot Head
Potted
Psychosing
Pumped
Riding the Magic Carpet
Riding the Wave
ROBO-ing

Rock Star (Being A...)	Toked Up
Rolling	Tooted
Roped	Tripped Out
Rushing	Tripping
Shot Gunned	Tuned Out
Shot the Breeze	Turned On
Shot Up	Tweaked Monster
Skinned	Tweaking
Skin-Popped	Twisted
Snapper	Veggin
Sneezed	Vipered
Sniffed	Wasted
Snorted	Waving
Snow-Birded	Whacked
Space Cadet	Wiped-Out
Spaced	Wired
Spaced Out	Zombie
Speed Balled	Zoned
Spun Out	Zoned Out
Steamrolled	Zoning
Stoked	Zonked
Stoned	Zooming
Strung Out	
Toasted	

Net Neutrality

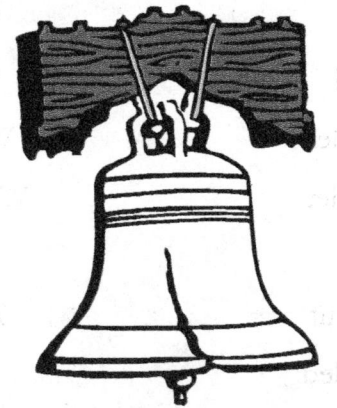

"The Code" may, at some time in the future, actually contain real code. Many countries are blacking out anything that they don't want their citizenry to know about. It is sad to say that many "Free" corporations are writing the programs that allow those countries to do just that. Some of these "Free" corporations are trying to control 'our' internet. That would be disastrous!

A word of caution: Don't be complacent; firmly oppose all threats to a free internet! NEVER let anyone or anything infringe on your right and freedom of the World-wide Web. Parents monitor your own children; NEVER allow the government to do so! Stop government regulations and internet taxes before they are imposed. Fight corporate manipulation and ownership. Fight the United Nation's attempts to gain management of the internet.

Freedom is seldom taken away in one fell swoop, it's usually taken the same way you eat an elephant… one bite at a time.

Does today's state of affairs in the world have you frustrated? "What can I do? I'm only one person." One way to help lessen your frustration is to join the fight to insure that the internet stays free. Now is the time to take a stand! Visit informative sites such as **www.savetheinternet.com** or **www.wearetheweb.org** and let your representatives in Congress know how you feel!

Keep the Internet Neutral and Free!

Text-Ers &
Instant Message-Ers

USA, DNA, UFO, HVAC, and other common acronyms not often used by Text-ers and I.M.-ers, are not included in "The Code".

If you feel strongly that your favorite AMASSED listing is not contained here, please contact us and we will make every attempt to have it included in our next printing.

Help Has Arrived!

Why don't kids understand parents, and parents understand kids? They don't really speak a different language. The new intergenerational language is internet and cellular text! You can bring everyone together...because you have

"THE CODE"

In today's fast paced world, everything has to be done NOW! No one has the time for elaborations, communication has to be succinct and to the point. As with everything, this too has evolved. You won't be left behind...because you have

"THE CODE"

For More Information on

"The Code"
and other

Handy Tabs Publications

visit us on the web at

www.handytabs.net

Share the Knowledge of

Are you perplexed by the shortcuts everyone uses for texting and instant messaging? That's why we created "The Code" ~ the quintessential easy reference you've been waiting for... in alphabetical order!

Payable by Check/Cashier's Check/Money Order/
PayPal (orders@handytabs.net)
"The Code" - $12.95
S&H - $3.00 for 1 book; $1.00 for each add.book
Call for international rates
Please allow 2-4 weeks for delivery

_____

Ship to:

Name:_____
Address:_____
City:_____ State:_____ Zip:_____
Phone:_____ Email:_____
Number of books:_____

_____

Mail to:
Handy Tabs, 4935 Spring Rd, Oak Lawn, IL 60453
708-422-3333

_____

Ask about Fundraising or Wholesale rates